Jersey Walks
for Motorists

F. de L. Bois

'Nor would we advise a stranger pressed for time to venture without a guide into the old country lanes, thoroughfares often delightful, but mysterious and treacherous, which start from nowhere and arrive nowhere, and which, once entered, he will know neither when nor by which way to come out.'

Translated from *Souvenirs de Jersey*
by Auguste Luchet

This edition published and printed 1992 by
The Guernsey Press Co Ltd, Guernsey, C.I.

By the same author
A Constitutional History of Jersey
The Parish Church of St Saviour, Jersey

Publishers' Note
While every care has been taken in the compilation of this book the
publishers cannot accept responsibility for any inaccuracies. Things may
have changed since the book was published: paths are sometimes diverted,
a concrete bridge may replace a wooden one, stiles disappear. Please let the
publishers know if you discover anything like this on your way.

The length of each walk in this book is given in miles and kilometres, but
within the text Imperial measurements are quoted. It is useful to bear the
following approximations in mind: 5 miles = 8 kilometres, $^1/_2$ mile = 805
metres, 1 metre = 39.4 inches.

Contents

ST. MARY

ST.

ST. LAWREN

0　　　1　　　2　　　3　　　4　　　5

0　　1　　2　　3　　4　　5　　6　　7　　8

6

JERSEY

THE NUMBERS SHOW WHERE THE WALKS START

Maps   The sketch maps which accompany each article are based on the Survey Maps produced for the Island Development Committee, whose kind permission to make use of them is here acknowledged.

Walkers are likely to save themselves much trouble in reaching the starting places of walks if they have the States of Jersey Official Map, Scale 1:25000.

The map grid references (SO Map references) indicating the starting places of walks consist of six figures in groups of three, each group locating imaginary lines, one vertical and one horizontal, whose intersection identifies the place required on the map. The first two figures refer to one of the vertical grid lines identified by a number to be found along the top and bottom of the map. The third figure represents tenths of the distance between that line and the next one to the right. Similarly the next two figures locate one of the horizontal grid lines, and the final one represents tenths of the distance between that line and the next one above. The locality required is thus within 50 metres of the intersection of the two imaginary lines obtained in this way.

Road names   The fact that the name of a road is given in the text does not necessarily mean that it is posted at the roadside.

Roadside parking places   These have been selected after consultation with the Constables of the parishes concerned. No special restrictions on parking in these places exist at the time of publication, but in any event, do not leave your car in a position likely to cause danger or obstruction. Leave plenty of room for the passage of farm machinery and other wide vehicles, and do not block field entrances, driveways, slipways and the like.

Churches   The walks pass close to eight of the parish churches. Walkers with sufficient time in hand are recommended to visit them.

Acknowledgement   I am grateful to many people for their assistance and advice, and I take this opportunity of renewing my thanks to them.

Note

In the course of the October 1987 hurricane, the handsome granite walls around many Jersey properties suffered badly through falling trees, and many V- or wedge-shaped repairs are to be seen — a notable example is the series of huge repairs on the roadside boundary of the Howard Davis Park in Don Road. Such scars, being pointed largely with new cement and sometimes reworked with stone from which the natural patina of that in the remaining wall has been abraded, are very obvious, and it may well be the turn of the century before they acquire the tone of the surrounding masonry. One good outcome of all this is that a new generation of stonemasons has been serving its apprenticeship to what was becoming a rare craft.

Glossary

Abreuvoir A watering place for animals taking the form of anything from a simple trough to something showy in dressed granite.

Buttes The name indicates the existence in former times of butts—a place where firing practices were held. The Island militia was for a long time based on the parish churches, and thus where the name *buttes* is found, there is a parish church not far away.

Constable The civic head of a parish

Don This word occurs quite frequently and generally has one of two meanings. If pronounced as in English, the reference is to General Don, Lieutenant-Governor of Jersey from 1806 to 1814; for example Don Road. If pronounced as in French, the word means gift, for example Don Jeanne Gruchy.

Don Jeanne Gruchy Stones recording this gift are to be found set into the roadside boundary walls of fields. Miss Gruchy was a lady of independent means from the parish of St John who died on 16 January 1848, aged 84 years and nine months, the cause of death being given as *vieillesse*. She bequeathed 1728 pounds (old French currency, worth one twenty-sixth of sterling) to the poorest inhabitants of the Island, directing that 144 pounds (£5.59) should be distributed by her executors at their discretion amongst the poor of each parish. She bequeathed her residuary personal estate to the twelve parishes in equal shares on condition that each parish should buy land with the legacy and use the annual rent to help poor people born in Jersey not regularly in receipt of relief. Her net residuary estate amounted to £7904 19s 9d (£7904.99).

Lavoir, Douet à Laver, Dou à Laver A place for washing household linen, usually built on the course of a stream *(douet* or *dou).*

Marriage Stones In the course of the walks, a number of what are commonly called marriage stones will be seen. The most popular form is a long rectangular block of granite with an inscription in incised or raised letters and figures, the stone very often serving as the lintel over the front door of a house. The inscription usually consists of a year—the first two figures on the left and the other two on the right—and in the centre two sets of initials separated by a dot, a colon, a single heart or two interlocking hearts. The date is sometimes set wholly on the left or right side of the stone, and is sometimes omitted. The initials are almost invariably those of

9

a married couple and consist of the most prominent letters of their names (for this purpose, the wife retains her maiden surname). For instance, Charles Mourant and Marie Cabot would be shown as CMR and MCB. The date is not necessarily that of the building of the house or of the marriage; it could be of some other important event. A dot between the initials is found on the earliest stones; later ones have a single heart and the latest have interlocking hearts. Instances of initials linked by an ampersand (&) are to be seen on Walks 8, 16 and 20. A rare example of a daisy head as the link in an inscription has regrettably been marred by the removal of the initials.

Milestones Milestones of simple design bearing only a figure, or a letter and a figure, result from a decision, made by the States on 16 November 1814 on the recommendation of the Lieutenant-Governor (Sir Tomkyns Hilgrove Turner), that suitable stones should be placed along all the Island's military roads. The distance was to be measured from the statue of King George II in the Royal Square. Generally speaking each series of stones has its own design, and the stones and their design enable one to recognise the course of the military roads created on the inspiration of another Lieutenant-Governor, General George Don, whose statue stands at the centre of The Parade, St Helier, and after whom the first military road to be established was named. A letter on the stone indicates the parish in which the stone stands.

Mounting blocks A number of mounting blocks are still to be seen by the roadside. They take the form of a flight of steps up to a small platform.

Parish road boundary stones These will be seen at the roadside on many of the walks. They vary from the modest to the magnificent and are a relic of the *corvée* system under which people were called on to repair the road of the vingtaines (see below) where they lived. Under a law of 1799, stones were placed to mark the boundaries and at the same time abolish any party roads. Where the boundary line passed along the centre of the road, one parish assumed responsibility for one stretch and the other assumed responsibility for the remainder.

Ville A group of houses.

Vingtaine Each of the twelve parishes is divided into vingtaines (called cueillettes in St Ouen's).

10

Walk 1
2 ½ miles (4 km)

Les Landes

Start: Grosnez Castle; SO Map ref. 550 565

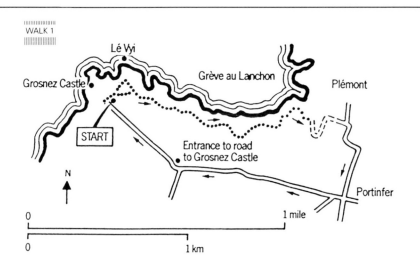

The north-west corner of Jersey is occupied by a considerable area of heath called 'Les Landes de Grosnez', formerly the Common of the branch of the Fief Haubert and Seigniory of St Ouen which belonged to Thomas Lemprière. (A fief haubert is one held *in capite*, that is to say, directly from the Crown, by homage and knight's service.)

There is adequate parking space close to Grosnez Castle, where this walk starts.

If the weather is favourable, Guernsey and Sark will be visible to the north with Herm and Jethou in between them. Sark is the closest to Jersey and is seen almost at its narrowest, with Little Sark nearer than the main part of the island. Guernsey, besides being much larger than Sark, looks larger in proportion because its south and east coasts are both visible

11

from Jersey. The French coast is away to the east; the Cotentin can be seen as far as Cap de la Hague when the air is exceptionally clear. Alderney, which stands off the cape, is also visible in clear weather.

Grosnez Castle was probably built in the early 14th century as a refuge for the inhabitants of the area and their livestock when the Island was raided. It is protected by steep cliffs on three sides, an idea of the protection afforded being shown by the cliff on the far side of the inlet to the west of the castle, La Noire Falaise or La Naithe Falaise. The word 'raided' is used advisedly, for there is no natural water supply to the castle and this alone would have made it difficult to withstand a prolonged siege.

There is a small quarry below the car park from where you will have a fine view down into the chasm Le Creux de la Moie, the upper part of which is known as Le Cottin Gavey or La Cotte ès Martins, and if the tide is sufficiently low, you will be able to see Le Pont de la Moie, the natural bridge which spans the mouth of the chasm.

Now find your way to the cliff path which leads east towards Plèmont. There is a seat where the path divides. The two forks soon rejoin, but the left fork provides the better view.

Below you is La Baie de la Vielle (The Bay of the Old Woman, named after a rock feature on the cliff) divided from Le Creux de la Moie by the headland called La Moie. Jutting out into the bay is a rock known as Le Vitré and at the right of the mouth of the bay, invisible from here but visible later on, Lé Vyi (The Old Man) stands guard.

You will not have gone very far before Plémont Point comes into view. The low seaward end, honeycombed with caves, is La Pièce Michel, and behind it is the headland Grand Plémont. Plémont itself stands to the east of La Grève au Lanchon, a bay

12

with a large sandy beach which takes its name from the sand-eels (*lanchons*) found there.

The path is well provided with seats, and after the second is passed it dips to cross the head of Le Creux des Maufaits (Lé Creux ès Maufaits). Extending down into this *creux* is the prominent outcrop called La Crête Rotchette (The Rocky Crest).

Between the second and third seats is a concrete platform, a relic of the German Occupation. From the third seat the path winds upwards to the right, with the houses at La Ville des Landes straight ahead, and then dips left to another well marked path which crosses from the right. This leads across the main cliff path and down La Vallette Haubert to the headland called La Cotte, the site of a paleolithic cave dwelling.

The path now dips steeply to the head of the declivity leading to the inlet known as Le Creux au Mouo and then climbs and turns sharply left and right, and left and right again, before reaching the fourth seat from where Plémont can be seen straight ahead. The path now twists upwards to skirt a hollow where, hidden in the undergrowth, are two springs, Les Fontaines Martin, and below them a *lavoir*. This was used by the women of the neighbourhood, La Ville des Landes, until the turn of the century.

After rounding the hollow, the path takes a turn to the right and follows the western side of La Grève au Lanchon, passing over unseen caves, La Cave ès Cormorans, La Cave du Tchêne and then three unnamed caves. La Cave du Tchêne is also known as La Longue Cave. It is a very long cave, but not nearly so long as it is reputed to be, for it is said to end under Portinfer, which you will pass on your return to Grosnez.

13

To the north-west a view of the coastline opens up showing Lé Vyi standing out from the base of the cliffs in the distance.

The path descends and ends at a short flight of steps in the trough of a valley, at the head of which is a modern house built on top of, and concealing, a German fortification.

Now turn to the right and follow the roadway leading up the side of the Plémont headland, and when you reach the top, look back for another view of Lé Vyi.

The track joins the road to the crossroads at Portinfer. When you reach the crossroads, turn right into La Rue du Val Bachelier which in slightly over half a mile will bring you to the road leading to Grosnez Castle. Some of the walling bordering the road merits more than a passing glance, for it incorporates heavy blocks of stone which superstitious people believe to be *pierres hantées* (haunted stones) derived from stone age monuments and possessed of magic powers. One wonders whether this is the reason for something up the road on the left near a bus stop (and opposite a farm entrance on the right), where a comparatively new wall, near its eastern end (you are approaching from the east), has been built round a large block of stone. Bearing this superstition in mind, is it not possible that the stone was left undisturbed so as to be on the safe side?

On the left further up the road, stones protrude from an old wall to act as steps for those wishing to climb it. A similar device is to be found in the wall opposite the entrance to the road to Grosnez Castle by which you will arrive back at your starting place.

3, 3 ¹/₂ and 6 miles (4.8, 5.6 and 9.7 km)

Start: For the 3 ¹/₂ and 6 mile walks, St Mary's Parish Hall;
SO Map ref. 602 543
For the 3 mile walk, beyond Crabbé Farm; SO Map ref. 593 555
The going along the cliff path is rough in places

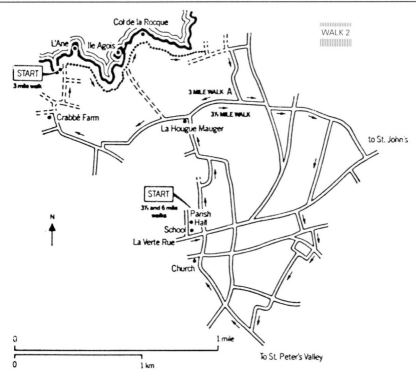

This article first describes the 6 mile walk. Details of the
alternative walks are given at the end. The 3 mile walk
includes the cliff path; the 3 ¹/₂ mile walk is wholly inland.

St Mary's Parish Hall is behind St Mary's School which
borders on La Verte Rue (B33). By kind permission of the
Constable of St Mary, walkers may park their cars in the
courtyard of the Parish Hall.

15

Turn left on leaving the Parish Hall, and turn left again on reaching the main road (La Verte Rue). Take the first turning to the left into a lane which leads into a marshy district appropriately called Les Marais. The lane turns to the right of the entrance to a house bearing that name, and on the right of the entrance the head of a (presumably roadside) cross is to be seen standing on a pillar which may well have come from St Mary's Church.

Just before the lane arrives at a T junction, there are some picturesque, though dilapidated, buildings. These provide a good example of a 19th-century practice of prosperous farmers who, devoting their profits to the building of new homes, did not demolish the old ones, but instead made use of them for storage. Observe also the mounting block on the right of the gateway.

At the T junction, turn to the left and thereafter continue ahead until a T junction is reached at La Hougue Mauger where the sea comes into view.

The mound called La Hougue Mauger no longer exists, having been destroyed on the building of the house bearing that name which stands on the western (left) side of the T junction. However, there remain on the site a number of unhewn stones with weathered surfaces built into the base of the boundary wall, and a broken quern at the top of the wall on the north-western corner.

Turn to the left and follow the lane until it ends at a T junction (passing on the way the head of a track on the right sign-posted 'Col de la Rocque'). St Peter's Mill is to be seen on the skyline to the south. Now turn to the right, ignore a lane which comes in on the left, and where the road divides take the branch to the right. The lane loses its tarmac surface at Crabbé Farm (on the left) and continues as a track which divides about 50 yards after it has taken a turn to the right. Take the left branch and continue ahead between gate pillars, passing the head of a bridle path on the right.

The cliff path is now reached and a view opens up to the west as far as Plémont with the butts of Crabbé rifle range in the foreground and Rouge Nez headland beyond.

COL DE LA ROCQUE CLIFF PATH, OVERLOOKING LES REUSES

The path turns to the right to follow the coast and takes a turn to the right on passing the headland known as L'Ane. The coast as far eastwards as Sorel comes into view with Ile Agois across the inlet below and Col de la Rocque behind it. The fact that Ile Agois is an island will become apparent as you proceed on your way. Recent researches show that it was intermittently occupied during the Iron Age and that a Christian settlement may have been established there during the Dark Ages. The path is easy to follow, but where the bridle path comes close, be careful not to be diverted on to it.

ILE AGOIS SHOWING ARCH AND TUNNEL

After having passed Ile Agois, the path leads to Col de la Rocque itself, an outcrop of rock forming a promontory. Immediately after the Col, steps lead downward and the Devil's Hole and the cliffs towards Sorel are now to be seen.

In due course you will come to a stile close to the head of a chasm, Les Reuses, to the foot of which there is a sheer fall of some 250 feet. Where the path rises and reaches a five-barred gate, pass through the gate and turn to the right. Then, at the top of the track, turn to the left and on arriving at the public highway, turn to the right. In slightly over a quarter of a mile there is a T junction (point A). Turn left and on arriving at another T junction, turn to the right and almost immediately to the left. After passing a crossroads, take the first turning to the right, which leads to the main road between St John's and St Mary's. On reaching the main road, turn to the right and then take the first turning to the left, which brings you to a T junction. Here turn to the left, then take the first turning to the right, and on arriving at a crossroads, go forward into the lane ahead. The lane shortly takes a turn to the right, after which the walk continues down the lane which comes in on the left.

Where in due course this lane takes a turn to the right, do not follow it. Instead, go ahead into what appears to be a cart track leading to a field. This is in fact a public road which has never been given a modern surface. As you enter it, look into the field on the left where you will see a row of low slender granite pillars, each with an iron rod protruding from the top. These are a form of post and rail fencing (called *les barres*) completed by placing wooden bars with holes at each end from pillar to pillar, the bars being held in place by rods passing through the holes.

On emerging on to the road (actually the road leading out of St Peter's Valley) turn to the right. At the top of the slope the road branches into two. The left branch will bring you to St Mary's Church.

In the nineteenth century, pillars obstructing the view of the pulpit were removed from this church and from the parish churches of Trinity and St John. In each case the pillar supported an arch on either side, and in every instance the single arch which resulted from this apparently perilous work has remained sound. At St Mary's the arch is at the eastern end of the church and a sight of it is recommended.

Continue ahead at the crossroads and then take the first turning to the left and the first turning to the right to arrive back at the Parish Hall.

3 mile walk Leave your car in the small car park beyond Crabbé Farm. Follow the route to point A and here turn right (instead of left). The lane leads to La Hougue Mauger where you continue ahead to follow the route back to your starting place.

3 ½ mile walk Follow the six mile route as far as La Hougue Mauger and here turn right (instead of left). The first turning to the left is point A: do not take it, but continue ahead and follow the remainder of the route.

Walk 3   Sorel

3 ½ miles (5.6km)

Start: Sorel car park; SO Map ref. 614 566
The path is steep in places

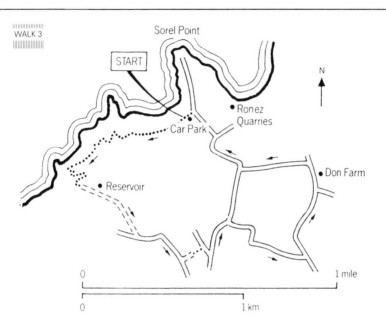

The car park is at the head of the cliff path which leads west from Sorel.

Before setting out, you may care to go as far as Sorel Point where there is a lighthouse. Directly ahead is the westernmost of the line of reefs which lie to the north and north-east of Jersey. Those to the north-east are the Dirouilles and the Ecrehos. This reef—the Paternosters or Les Pierres de Lecq— measures about 1 ½ miles from east to west and a little over a mile from north to south at low spring tides. At high tide there is little evidence of the danger which lies beneath; hence the

21

appropriateness of the name Paternosters, for mariners need the protection of the Almighty when adrift in these waters. The Island of Sark can, except in thick weather, be seen on the horizon beyond the Paternosters.

Immediately to the east of the Sorel headland are Ronez quarries whose expansion led, in 1978, to the coast road being resited further inland.

Set out westwards along the cliff path at the foot of the car park. The headland in the far distance is Plémont. The path takes a switch-back course following the contours of the coast with unavoidable exceptions which make it steep in places. Look back while Sorel Point is still in view and observe the cliff face with its granite strata of different colours.

The path eventually arrives above Mourier Valley and takes a zig-zag course downhill. On reaching the foot of the path, turn left and go along the track up the valley. The reservoir and pumping station to the left of the track are part of the Island's public water supply system.

At the top of the track, a road descends from a hill to the right, and a little further on the valley brook appears, running in an open channel along the left side of the road. In about 100 yards, just past the point where the brook emerges from a culvert, there is a track leading off to the left with a well head on the far side of it.

Go up this track and on passing London House on the left, take note of the marriage stone which serves as the lintel of the front door. It is unusual in that the date, 1842, is between the initials of the husband and wife (Edouard Ahier and Esther d'Auvergne) and it is even more unusual in that the Christian name of the husband is shown as an abbreviation (Ed) instead of a single initial.

Continue along the track which narrows into a footpath and rises steeply up the hillside, joining a track towards the top. Where shortly the track emerges onto the public highway, turn to the right and in about 50 yards, bear left. The road rises slightly and where it divides, bear right. The television mast of the Independent Broadcasting Authority is on the horizon directly ahead. The road takes a turn to the right and a turn to the left and in due course arrives at a small built-up area where the walk continues to the left round a hairpin bend. About 100 yards beyond the point where a road comes in on the right is Don Farm whose attractive frontage is of a date much earlier than most now to be seen in Jersey. In 1913, two magnificent open fireplaces were discovered, one on the ground floor and one on the first floor. Many years later they were found lying in an outhouse under a heap of turnips. They were bought by the Société Jersiaise.

Where the lane divides, take the left fork which in due course brings you to a T junction where the walk continues to the right. The first turn to the left leads you back to Sorel, giving you, if the weather is favourable, a further view of the Paternosters and the Island of Sark. It may be that the tide has receded while you were on your walk, making the extent of the Paternosters more apparent. Or it may be that you will see the Paternosters at low tide when the sea is rough. The perils of the reef will then be obvious.

Walk 4   **St John's**

3 ¹/₄ and 4 ¹/₄ miles (5.2 and 6.8 km)

Start: Mont Mado; SO Map ref. 639 553

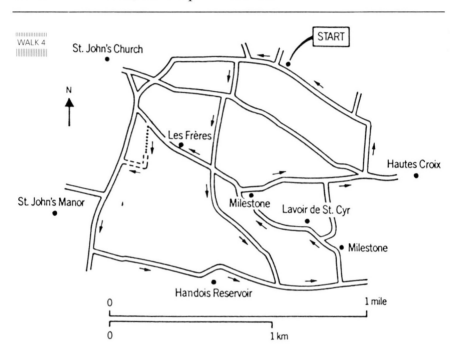

This walk starts at Mont Mado, the miscellany of ancient, modern and modernized houses south of the abandoned quarries whose granite of fine grain and warm colour makes many of the Island's buildings so attractive.

La Route du Mont Mado runs north of and parallel to the main road between Hautes Croix and St John's Church, and you should have no difficulty in finding a suitable place in it to park your car.

Set out in a westerly direction, and as you pass the last house but one on the right, note a good example of a marriage

24

stone serving as the lintel of its entrance doorway. It bears the date 1721, the initials CLG and TP, and a single heart between the initials.

Take the first turning to the left into a lane which will bring you to the main road between Hautes Croix and St John's Church. Turn right up the main road and almost immediately turn left into a lane. The lane ends at cross-roads where you have the choice of two alternative routes.

First alternative Continue ahead down La Rue du Pont, an attractive lane passing across two shallow valleys. At the beginning of the second valley, a beautiful conservatory in the Victorian style is to be seen on the property to the left of the road and also a random stone wall luxuriously curved to accommodate the trees lining it. Both constructions are of recent date.

The lane mounts and ends at a T junction where the second alternative route comes in on the right. Turn therefore to the left. (For the remainder of the walk see page 26.)

Second alternative At the crossroads, turn to the right. Soon you will reach Les Frères Methodist Church (now the headquarters of the Boys' Brigade), with an older chapel at its side, their quiet dignity in no way recalling the turbulent foundation of Methodism in Jersey when the followers of the Wesley brothers were considerably harassed by the authorities, mainly because of their refusal to serve in the militia, service being then compulsory.

The origin of the name 'Les Frères' is uncertain, but it is likely that the chapel was called after the brothers John and Charles Wesley.

About 300 or 400 yards beyond Les Frères there is a grassy pathway on the left of the road, along which the walk continues. Towards the end the path becomes a cart track and turns to the right where it acquires a tarmac surface and emerges onto the main road to St John's Church. Now turn to the left and in about a quarter of a mile you will reach the entrance to St John's Manor (Le Manoir de St Jean de la Hougue Boëte).

About 100 yards after the manor entrance, turn left into Le Huchet (Le Hucquet; Lé Hutchet) which later changes its name to La Rue de la Scelleterie. It passes the head of Handois Reservoir which now drowns the Rosemount china-stone quarry where in about 1866 a rock was discovered which was harder and somewhat finer-grained than most of the Cornish china-stones and much less kaolinized. The product was marketed at about half the price charged by a Cornish association, with the result that in a few years the association was disbanded and the price of Cornish stone fell. All the stone was shipped out of the Island, and a reminder of the trade will be found at the top of the hill as you continue on your way. On the left of the road is an open space which now serves as a passing place. The stone is exceedingly heavy, and a cart drawn by two horses could carry no more than half a load from the quarry to the top of the rise. The stone was then dumped and the horses and cart would fetch another half load. Returning to the top of the rise, the first half load would be reloaded and the stone then taken to St Helier for export.

Further on, where there is a building on the right of the road, a parish road boundary stone will be found in the bank on the left which bears the letters St L and St J on opposite faces, indicating the parishes of St Lawrence and St John. The road which comes in on the left is La Rue du Pont.

The routes reunited Continue ahead and take the first turning to the left into La Rue des Chenolles. It is an appropriately named road. *Chenolle* is the Jersey equivalent of the French *manivelle*–a crank or winch–and thus fits a road such as this which turns like a series of cranks laid end to end.

After the first turn to the left and before the first turn to the right, observe the four-mile stone on the right of the road.

Soon, on the right of the road, there is a fine *lavoir* and fountain–Le Douet de St Cyr. To its north is a lime kiln (*four à chaux; fou à chaux*) in which shells were burnt to provide lime. This was a necessary process as Jersey has no natural limestone. The lime kiln is accessible only to members of the Société Jersiaise and their guests, but another is to be seen at the Jersey Zoo.

In due course La Rue des Chenolles takes a turn to the left and is joined by a road on the right. The steps set into the wall for access to the field above make an interesting comparison with the more primitive version at the end of Walk I (p.14). This is La Rue Militaire along which the walk continues. A short way up it, set into the wall on the right, is a five-mile stone. You may be puzzled because the four-mile stone in La Rue des Chenolles is only half a mile away. The explanation is that the course of the military road marked by the stones followed St John's Main Road to Hautes Croix and thence west, resulting in there being a three-mile stone north of Sion, a four-mile stone south of Hautes Croix, and then the five-mile stone.

Where La Rue Militaire joins the main road between Hautes Croix and St John's Church, observe the stone set into a wall on the far side of the road. This marks one of the two *Clos des Pauvres* of the parish of St John, resulting from the gift of Miss Jeanne Gruchy.

Cross the main road to La Route du Mont Mado. Mont Mado lies ahead.

Walk 5   Les Platons and Ville-à-l'Evêque
3 miles (4.8 km)

Start: Trinity Parish Hall; SO Map ref. 662 542

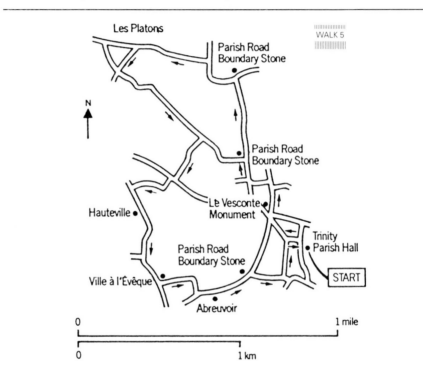

The next two walks start from Trinity Parish Hall where, by kind permission of the Constable, walkers may park their cars.

Set out from the Parish Hall along the main road in the direction of Hautes Croix (west). You will soon reach Les Croix where five roads meet. Here stands the Le Vesconte Monument; it commemorates Philippe Le Vesconte, Constable of Trinity from 1868 to 1877 and 1890 to 1909. Take the second road to the right (La Rue du Tas de Géon) which leads northwards towards Les Platons.

28

HIGHEST POINT, LES PLATONS, TRINITY

In about 250 yards you will come to the first turning to the left. Take it and follow the road where in about 150 yards it turns to the right.

Where a lane comes in on the left about 100 yards further on, there is a parish road boundary stone at the foot of the bank on the northwest side of the corner. Following the usual practice, the initials are the predominant letters of the names of the vingtaines concerned, and one has here a set of initials which are quite unusual. The vingtaines are Rondin and Ville-à-l'Evêque. The first, as one would expect, is represented by RD. The second, however, contains an example of the selection of predominant letters rather than the first letter of syllables—Ville-À-L'éVêque—and a combination of the letters A and L.

Continue ahead to a T junction where you will find another parish road boundary stone set into the top of the wall immediately in front of you. Turn to the left and follow the road to the west, taking care not to go into the lane ahead where the road takes a turn to the left. Some way beyond the turn, you will come to a lane on the left; the high land to the right is the highest part of Jersey. Go along the lane and when the crossroads are reached, turn left into a narrower lane.

Not far along on the left of the lane, the second property is an L-shaped house which has recently been restored, making it somewhat difficult to see the lintel of a window facing the road near the corner of the L. It bears an inscription which could possibly be a reminder of a long forgotten tragedy. On the left are the figures 17 and on the right the figures 63. There is nothing in between. Could it be that some eager betrothed of 1763 started carving his marriage stone in anticipation of a wedding which never took place? Or maybe marriage kept the bridegroom too busy to complete his handiwork.

The lane twists and turns and then runs straight, and about a quarter of a mile from the crossing it passes a farm house, Les Ormes, where until the recent fencing of the front garden a fine well-head could be seen. The outbuilding is dated 1772, the garden gate 1897, and the marriage stone above the front door 1765. The single heart on the marriage stone (between the initials ILM and EDG) is drawn in outline, and contrasts with another to be seen later in this walk.

In another 200 to 250 yards, turn right into a lane which ends at a T junction. Here turn right and very shortly turn left into another lane. After a mild descent, this lane turns to the right, crosses a shallow valley and ends at a T junction where you turn to the left. Just beyond the corner on the right is a house, La Hocquarderie, the front of which holds a marriage stone with the inscription in raised letters and figures and (contrasting with the stone at Les Ormes) a single heart carved solid.

The lane swings to the right and rises. Near the top of the rise, the field entrance to the left gives a wide view over the valley towards Ebenezer Methodist Church on the skyline.

The farmyard entrance to the next house on the right, Hauteville, is worthy of attention, constructed as it is of alternate bands of red and blue granite blocks.

When the lane takes a turn to the right, look back, towards Hauteville where you will see a farm bell hung within a chimney stack, something which, if not unique, must be very rare.

Follow the lane as it slopes gently downhill and bears to the left, passing an indoor riding school on the left of the road. Just beyond, there is a roadside wall with a blocked up doorway. The lintel has been left in position and bears the date 1796 with the initials PNC and MLQ on either side of two interlocking hearts.

Soon comes a lane on the left along which the walk continues. A little way down the lane, on the left, is a magnificent double arched farmyard entrance. The arms and motto (Au valeureux coeur rien impossible), beautifully carved on the granite tablet above the pedestrian doorway, attract immediate attention, but the unusual heart-shaped plate of the handle of the door below should not be overlooked.

The lane eventually ends at a T junction where you turn to the left. A little further on is a large *abreuvoir public* on the right of the road, and a little way beyond, on the same side, there is a marriage stone, with the date 1825, the initials JNC and IAM and two interlocking hearts, serving as the lintel of a window.

Where the road forks, the southernmost of the four parish road boundary stones between Rondin and Ville-à-l'Evêque will be found at the foot of the wall on the left.

Take the right fork. Some way along the road there is a stone basin built into the wall on the left. The basin serves no purpose where it is now set; it could well be a piscina designed for the ablutions of the priest's hands and of the chalice and paten at mass. Piscinas were usually placed on the south side of the altar, and possibly this one came from Trinity Church.

The first turning to the left, followed by the first turning to the right, will bring you back to the Parish Hall.

Walk 6   **The environs of Trinity Church**

3 miles (4.8 km)

Start: Trinity Parish Hall; SO Map ref. 662 542 (see Walk 5)

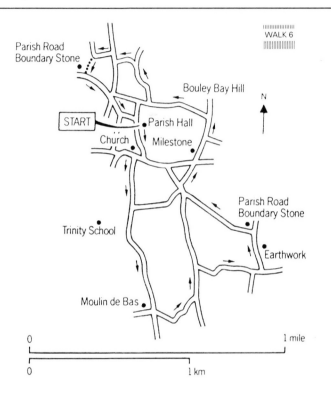

On leaving the Parish Hall, turn left towards Trinity Church. When the road ends at a T junction, turn right and then take the first turning to the left into a lane opposite the south entrance to the churchyard. A visit to the church is recommended for a sight of the tremendous arch on the north side of the chancel, a feature shared with the parish churches of St Mary (see p. 16) and St John.

On one side of the south entrance to the churchyard is the

33

Parish Poor Box above which is the inscription 'Fais l'aumône de tes biens. Ne détourne point ta face du pauvre et la face du Seigneur ne sera point détournée de toi'. (Give of your goods in alms. Turn not your face from the poor and the face of the Lord will not be turned from you.)

The lane opposite the south entrance leads off to the south, down into one of the arms of the main valley of the Grands Vaux. As you descend, you will see Trinity School (known in the old days as Lé Collège) on your right and further on you will come to a fine granite double entrance gateway on the left of the road. This, the entrance to Mont Pellier, is not the original gateway, but one from The Hollies in La Rue de la Croix, St Clement.

At the foot of the lane you come to a crossroads. On your right is a dwelling-house, formerly a watermill, Le Moulin de Bas, and on your left a wooded slope, Le Don Huelin, the property of the National Trust for Jersey. Turn to the left up a hill and when you reach the top, turn left at a T junction. In 150 to 200 yards turn right into a lane which will bring you to a farm called Les Câteaux. At the left of the entrance is a mounting block with steps on both sides. Above the mounting block is a stoup and over the stoup a stone engraved with the initials PHM and MBP and a date, the first three figures of which are 169. A stoup is a basin near the entrance of a church containing holy water with which the faithful may sprinkle themselves, and it is possible that, having ceased to be of use in the parish church as a consequence of the Reformation, it was discarded as redundant when works of reconstruction were carried out.

Turn left up the lane just beyond the entrance to Les Câteaux. Shortly you will come to the earthwork, on the right of the lane, from which the farm derives its name. It was constructed in the Middle Ages as a bank and ditch enclosure for the protection of people and their animals when the Island was raided. The same earthwork is also the source of the name of Le Câtel Farm on the left further up the lane.

Turn to the left into the lane in front of Le Câtel Farm, and at the corner note the parish road boundary stone in a recess at the foot of the roadside wall. This bears the letters RD and RZ which denote the Trinity vingtaines of Rondin and Rozel.

The lane winds and where it ends, turn right and shortly right again into a road which leads gently uphill. On the left is an odd-shaped building (in the form of a trapezium) which used to accommodate schools for boys and girls and also served as an Independent Chapel.

At the crossroads proceed ahead and in about 80 yards you will come to a four-mile stone set into the bank on the left, one of a series of five, the second of which is to be seen on Walk 12. The fifth stone is at the foot of Bouley Bay Hill.

The road continues to rise for a short way, and when you reach the top of the rise pause, for here the slope of the land upwards from the south coast ends and turns to fall sharply to the sea on the north coast which is visible not very far in front of you.

The walk continues up the first turning to the left and then down the first turning to the right. The lane descends, winds and then mounts steeply to emerge onto a road where the latter passes through a broad curve. Follow the curve to the left, continuing uphill, the slope lessening as you proceed. The road ends at a T junction, joining the main road leading to Les Platons. At this point, turn to the right, and about 50 yards up the road, turn to the left and go straight on to what appears to be a crossroads. Actually the road along which you have come goes off to the right and the road to the left is a dead end. Your way lies ahead towards a farm house with an open carriage entrance and an arched pedestrian entrance on its left which has the inscription 1663, IM and a fleur-de-lys on the keystone of the arch.

At the farm house, turn left into a footpath. This will bring you to the main road between Trinity Church and Hautes Croix. A cavity at the foot of the wall on the right holds a stone which, on examination, proves to be a parish road boundary stone between the Trinity vingtaines of Rondin and Ville-à-l'Evêque. The stone is one of a series similarly marked to be seen on Walk 5. This stone is unlike any other stone of the series in that it has additional letters on its face, the initials (ILBTL and IMC) designating Jean Le Boutillier and Jean Machon who were Roads Inspectors of the Vingtaine du Rondin at the end of the 18th and the beginning of the 19th centuries.

Now turn to the left in the direction of Trinity Church. The monument on your left when you reach the crossroads at which five roads meet commemorates Philippe Le Vesconte, Constable of Trinity from 1868 to 1877 and 1890 to 1909. Continue straight ahead, leaving two roads on your left and one on your right. The road soon curves left to bring you back to the Parish Hall.

Walk 7

Above Bouley Bay

2 miles (3.2 km)

Start: Jardin d'Olivet; SO Map ref. 670 542
There is a fairly stiff climb to the top of Bouley Bay Hill

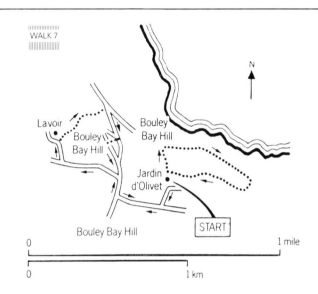

Le Jardin d'Olivet or La Commune du Fief de la Gruchetterie is to the east of the top of Bouley Bay Hill. Park your car here.

Take the road leading south from the western end of the Common and at the T junction which you will shortly reach, turn right. Turn right again at another T junction which lies about 250 yards ahead and then take the first turning to the left. The road rises passing the Common of the Fief de l'Abbesse de Caen on its right.

The Fief of the Abbess of Caen is now a Crown Fief, having been seized by King Henry V in 1413 together with the Channel Islands' possessions of all other French religious houses. There was then a split in the Papacy. England

37

supported one side and France the other, and the English king took advantage of the situation.

Proceed westwards along the road until you reach a lane leading off to the right. Go down this lane, but before doing so, observe the long strip of land on the left of the road beyond the mouth of the lane. This results from the road having been driven straight ahead, isolating the strip which was originally part of the field on the other side of the road. Strips of this nature, called *issues*, are to be found at the end of Walk 21 and in other parts of Jersey. This strip, Le Don Le Breton, belongs to the National Trust for Jersey.

At the foot of the lane, you will come to a private drive (to La Petite Brunerie and La Brunerie), on the left of which is a footpath. The route continues down this footpath which will shortly bring you to the entrance to a wooded hillside, le Grand Côtil du Boulay, belonging to the National Trust for Jersey. On the left, just before the entrance to the National Trust property, is Lé Puchot. In Jersey *puchot* means a rough fountain or water source in the form of a pool, and here you will find a stream running through a paved enclosure containing a *lavoir*. At its side is a random stone wellhead fronted with a wrought iron gate. A similar wellhead and gate stand about 40 yards away at the head of the track to the right.

The path through the National Trust property leads downhill and will bring you to a hairpin bend on Bouley Bay Hill. At this point, proceed uphill to the right, and in about 100 yards, just after the woodland ends, another *lavoir* is to be found on the bank to the right of the road. The *lavoir* stands on another part of the Common of the Fief de l'Abbesse de Caen and is said to have still been in use in the early part of this century.

Continue uphill to the next hairpin bend where the road

divides, the main road going off to the right and a steeper road continuing straight ahead. This latter served to give access to a Guard House on the left of the road, and now it serves a useful purpose in the motor vehicle races which take place up the main road. Known as the slip road, it is so called because when all the vehicles have raced to the top of the hill, they are brought down it, and thence to the bottom of the hill, to start all over again.

Do not go up either road but mount the steep path and steps which lie between them. It is a pity that your back will be to the view. However you will be glad to pause on your way. The view to the east needs no recommendation; on the skyline to the north you will see the three tall masts of the Decca Navigator Station, one of a number of transmitting beacon stations erected in the British Islands and the Continent of Europe by means of which ships specially equipped for the purpose may ascertain their exact position. At the top of the hill somewhat to the right are the ruins of a Guard House, Les Hurets, and in the hollow between the masts and the Guard House is a black hut erected by the Germans during the Occupation.

At the top of the steps, continue ahead to Bouley Bay Hill where there is a flight of steps on the far side of the road with a quarry to its left. The whitish stone of this quarry, used for the repair of the roads of the parish of Trinity before the days of tarmac, made those roads entirely characteristic and unlike the roads of any other parish. The stone is actually volcanic ash.

Going up the hill, turning left and left again will bring you back to your starting place.

The paths through the Jardin d'Olivet and the adjoining common (la Commune du Fief de Diélament) provide a very pleasant walk.

Start in the north-west corner where, hidden among the trees, you will find the remains of a Victorian gazebo built expressly for the enjoyment of the view over Bouley Bay, a view now obscured by trees.

Set out to the east along the seaward border of the common, choosing paths that do not lead too far down the hillside. First you will have a fine view of Bouley Bay Harbour within the small bay called Porteret, of the cliffs to the north towards Vicard Point and of the steep valley to the north-west through which Bouley Bay Hill is carved.

Continuing along the top of the slopes you will eventually come to a deep valley, and you will have to turn inland. In the near distance across the valley is the massive outcrop La Tête des Hougues. Beyond, above the rocks which lie at the foot of the cliff, is L'Etaquerel Fort, and in the distance, enclosing the eastern end of the bay, is La Tour de Rozel.

The valley curves round the back of the common and its lush vegetation is in startling contrast to the gorse and heather of the common itself. A hut erected by the Germans during the Occupation can be seen on the farm on the far side of the valley.

A track runs up the valley. Find a path descending to it which you are willing to negotiate, for to return by this track provides a delightful walk. Some way up the valley, the track divides, but the division is only a loop of which the lower part is the more attractive. The track leads to the open common from where you set out.

Walk 8   Rozel and Saie Harbour

3 miles (4.8 km)

Start: La Chasse Fleurie, St Martin; SO Map ref. 704 535
The route follows a switchback course involving hills of
varying steepness

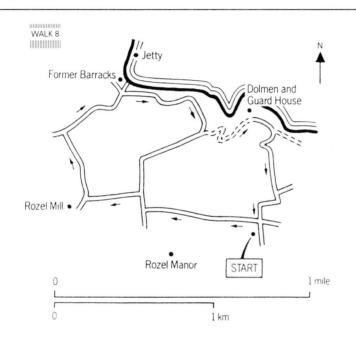

The crossroads above the north-east corner of the Island lead
to St Martin's Church (B91), Saie Harbour, Fliquet Bay and St
Catherine's Bay (B91). The road to St Catherine's Bay (La
Chasse Fleurie) begins by running south straight and wide
from the crossroads, and it is in this part of the road that
walkers should park their cars.

The walk starts in the direction of St Martin's Church
westward along La Rue des Pelles. There are roads of the same
name in the parishes of St Ouen and Trinity, and *pelle* is a fairly

FLIQUET BAY

common field name, indicating one which has been cleared for cultivation. As you near the end of the road, you will see Rozel Manor across the field to the left.

La Rue des Pelles ends at a T junction on the far side of which stands a house whose stonework is entirely of dressed granite. Turn right at the T junction and shortly turn left into La Rue de Caen from which the top of Rozel Mill appears over the houses to the left ahead, showing how the Germans adapted it during the Occupation to serve as an observation post.

Turn to the right at the end of La Rue de Caen to descend a steep hill. Near the foot of the hill is a small fountain set into the garden wall on the left. About 25 yards further on, the house at the corner of the road has a marriage stone serving as the lintel of the front door. The incised inscription is dated 1797 and the initials PDF and IN are linked by a single heart.

The road now turns to the right and passes through a narrow valley planted with mimosa, rhododendrons, camelia, conifers, palms and magnolia. There is another door lintel marriage stone on the house to the left where the road through the valley joins that which crosses Rozel Bay. The stone has an incised inscription dated 1826 with the initials ILG and ERN linked by interlocking hearts.

The walk continues up the hill to the right, but first go ahead for a view of the bay, with its harbour built in 1829 to shelter the large number of oyster boats using it as a mooring place. The building to your left originated as Rozel Barracks in the early 19th century when Jersey was considered to be in imminent danger of invasion by the French. The frontage on the beach remains largely in its original state.

Should you choose to cross the beach to the harbour, you will see an unusual inscription on a marriage stone above the front door of the house half way down the approach road to the jetty. Dated 1832, the initials JRS and JLS are linked, not by the usual heart or interlocking hearts, but by an ampersand (&) tilted backwards.

Now continue up the hill to the east from which there is a good view of the bay. The peculiar table-like construction on the headland which could be taken to be of megalithic origin is, in fact, part of a German fortification.

At the summit of the hill the road makes a right-angled turn and then runs straight. A little way beyond the turn, there is an entrance to a track, La Rue des Fontenelles (the road of the little springs), which comes in at an acute angle on the seaward side of the road.

Follow the track downhill into a lonely valley, watered by a brook which empties into a tiny cove. As you mount the track out of the valley, a view of the cliffs west of Rozel opens up, with a restricted view into Rozel Harbour.

Soon after the track begins to descend towards Saie Harbour, you will find a field entrance on the left which leads to Le Dolmen de Couperon, a long cist or *allée couverte*. It was first excavated and restored in 1868, since when further work has been done to put it in order. An interesting stone is that at the eastern end of the cist, which has a half circle carved out of it. The stone was placed there during a restoration in 1919, but one cannot say with certainty that it was restored to its original position. The building beside the dolmen was formerly a Guard House.

From the nearby hill there is a fine view west into Rozel Bay and east into Saie Harbour, with the headland, La Coupe Point, at its far end. Saie Harbour is the easternmost bay on the northern coast and the headland forms the north-east corner of the Island. The tower on La Coupe Point used to be a Royal Navy look-out post.

Go down into the bay itself to see the cart track carved out of the rock to provide access to the beach, principally for the removal of *vraic* (pronounced 'wrack'), a seaweed used for feeding the soil.

Part of the land bordering the bay belongs to the National Trust for Jersey, its eastern end being marked by the tree-crowned prominence about half way along the bay which bears the name Le Nid ès Corbins (The Crow's Nest).

Take the road out of the bay and when you arrive at the crossroads, your walk is complete.

Walk 9
4 miles (6.4 km)

In the heart of St Ouen's

Start: St Ouen's Church car park; SO Map ref. 579 531

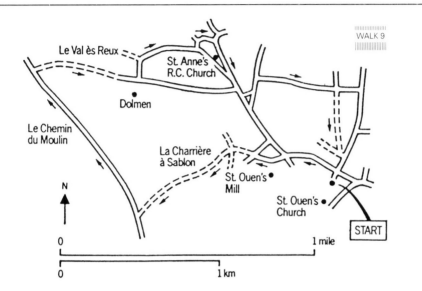

The next two walks start from St Ouen's Church where there is a car park to the north of the churchyard. By kind permission of the Rector and Churchwardens, walkers may park their cars there.

At the end of the lane giving access to the car park, turn left into La Rue de la Cour. The remains on the right of the lane are part of the Batterie Ludendorff, built by the Germans during the Occupation and armed with three 21 cm Morser 18 medium howitzers. The bunker blocked the road, as did another in La Chasse de l'Eglise (the continuation of the access lane to the car park).

When you reach the end of La Rue de la Cour, you will see the tower of a windmill on the skyline to the left ahead. This is all that remains of St Ouen's Mill or Le Moulin de la Campagne which the Germans capped with concrete and used as an observation tower for the Batterie Ludendorff.

Now continue ahead into a lane with a rough surface which leads to Lowlands, formerly known as L'Abreuvoir, and follow it as it curves to the right and then goes slightly uphill. At its end cross the road to a track along which the walk continues and which leads past Le Clos du Farrouin to the head of La Charrière à Sablon.

Le Farrouin (which has the same derivation as the French word *phare*: a lighthouse) preserves the name, *Lé Fârouîn*, of the place where a beacon was lit to aid navigators. It was also one of the last look-out points for those watching sailing ships carrying their relatives and friends on their way westwards to La Côte (the Gaspé Coast, and by extension, the coasts of Newfoundland and Labrador).

Where you emerge onto open country, the track divides. One branch continues ahead, another goes off to the left, and between the two there is a narrow track leading down into St Ouen's Bay. This is La Charrière (or La Tchithiéthe) à Sablon—well named, for it is both an unmade track and sandy; as the sides have fallen in however it is no longer suitable for the passage of carts.

La Charrière à Sablon leads down to Les Hanières, so called after the *han* (*Cyperus longus* or sweet galingale) which grew here. This coarse grass, which could easily cut one's hand, was once used for making such things as cord, matting, halters and horse collars. It was also used for binding sheaves when there was insufficient straw.

At this point the track takes the name of Le Chemin des Hanières and leads on to Le Chemin du Moulin where it ends at a T junction.

Le Chemin du Moulin was the mill road which served *Les Etac 'sos* (the inhabitants of L'Etacq) when taking their corn for grinding at Le Moulin de la Mare, the water mill at the foot of Mont Rossignol, or Le Moulin de la Campagne, the windmill at the top of the hill.

At Le Chemin du Moulin, turn right. The road runs straight and is well lined with houses, the last of which on the right is called La Rocque à l'Aigle after an outcrop of rock which once stood on the site. Just before reaching the house, turn right into a grassy track which passes up the hill through Le Val ès Reux. Beyond the top of the hill the track acquires a tarmac surface and about 50 yards further on there is a lane on the left and a field entrance on the right. Across the field within a surrounding wall, lies a passage-grave known as Le Dolmen des Monts, Grantez, the property of the Société Jersiaise. An alternative name for the passage-grave is La Pouquelaye des Monts. When it was excavated in 1912, remains of skeletons were found, but they were too fragmentary to be of any value.

Turn to the left into the lane opposite the field entrance and follow it to the right where a track comes in on the left. Eventually you will reach a place where the road forks. Take the left fork to skirt the field in front. The road slopes gently downwards and again forks, the right fork being the one to take. Where the road curves to the left, it is crossed by a stream which is headed, on the right of the road, by La Fontaine d'Auvergne.

Across the field on the left is a long single storeyed house in fine condition which shows clear signs of having originated as a German hut during the Occupation.

As you complete the circuit of the field, you will come to St Anne's Roman Catholic Church on the right of the road. The building does not look at all like a church; it looks like a school, which indeed it was, for it originally housed the Westwood Training College.

Turn left into a short lane and, at its end, turn again to the left. On the far side of this turning is an *abreuvoir* fed by a small stream which emerges from a culvert and continues in an open channel along the side of the road. About 100 yards ahead, turn to the right into La Rue à l'Eau, along the right side of which the stream feeding the *abreuvoir* is again to be seen running in an open channel.

The walk continues along the first turning to the right, a track which, towards its end, passes through more of the remains of the Batterie Ludendorff.

Turn left where the track joins another at a T junction and turn right where it emerges onto a road, La Chasse de l'Eglise. The church now lies directly ahead.

Walk 10

South of St Ouen's Church

3 ½ miles (5.6 km)

Start: St Ouen's Church car park; SO Map ref. 579 531 (see Walk 9)

There is a steep hill on this walk. Part of the way may be muddy

---

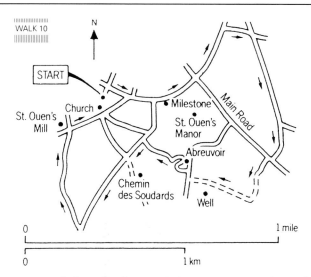

Leave the car park by the lane giving access to it and take the first turning to the right into La Rue de la Cour, and where it joins the eastern end of La Ville de l'Eglise, continue ahead. The road soon takes the name of La Rue du Manoir. Some way up it, gates on the right lead into the grounds of St Ouen's Manor, and about 25 yards beyond the gates there is a milestone bearing the letter O (for St Ouen) and the number six. This stone is one of a series which follows St Aubin's Road and Old Beaumont Hill, as neither Victoria Avenue nor New Beaumont Hill were built at the time when the stones were set up.

49

Cross the main road (La Grande Route de St Ouen) into La Rue du Douet and take the first turning to the right into La Rue de la Mare Cauchez, and again the first turning to the right into La Verte Rue. In due course, you will come to a lane on the left opposite a farm house on the right. When you come to the next farm house on the right, La Verte Rue Farm, observe the lintel of the front door—a marriage stone with a somewhat unusual inscription. The date 1759 is arranged on either side of the interlocking hearts, the initials of the husband and wife being outermost.

La Verte Rue emerges onto the main road. Here turn to the right and in about 40 yards turn left into La Ruette du Coin. As you proceed down La Ruette du Coin, you will see, on your right, Les Huriaux Farm, with an entrance of unusual design and a dwelling-house of typical Jersey style, equally typically masking buildings of a much earlier date.

Further on, the tarmac surface comes to an end. On the right is the entrance to Le Coin Farm (formerly La Maison du Coin) and on the left is the continuation of La Ruette du Coin which was reopened in 1965 after having been blocked by the Germans during the Occupation.

The lane runs gently downhill, to continue close to, and parallel with, the track to Val de la Mare reservoir on its left. Shortly it rises, taking a turn to the right, and assumes the name of Les Ruelles. At the top of the rise, a farm track is crossed and about 300 yards further on there is a field on the left near the centre of which is a good example of an old Jersey well, with a sill at its mouth for resting the bucket.

Les Ruelles emerges onto La Rue du Coin which serves the district known as Le Coin. This is an area apart, which at one time had almost the standing of a cueillette (St Ouen is divided into cueillettes—other parishes into vingtaines). It had its own militia company, called Les Cracots du Coin after the black buttons of their uniform and the *vraic* (seaweed) of that name which the buttons resembled.

On entering La Rue du Coin turn right and you will soon come to something of interest on the right of the road. Bearing the date 1898 and the names of the Constable and members of the Roads Committee of the parish, it was clearly intended to be a fountain. However, it has remained nothing more than an ornament, for the expectation that water would collect in it from the field above, Le Clos de la Montagne, has never been fulfilled.

Now turn left into Les Charrières du Coin, known simply as Les Tchithiéthes. A *charrière* was originally an unmade road—a cart track—of which examples are to be found elsewhere. Nowadays, however, the name is found applied to districts and metalled roads.

The road soon takes a turn to the right and descends into a deep valley at the foot of which there is a small *abreuvoir* on the right where the brook passes under the road.

Now comes a steep hill out of the valley which continues as La Rue de la Croute and ends at a T junction. The walk continues to the left along La Rue des Pelles. On the right of the road there is an example of an old Jersey farm house, Les Ormes, which has been demolished and rebuilt in another position.

Le Mont Rossignol (so named after the Le Rossignol family and not because it is a haunt of nightingales) is a continuation from La Rue des Pelles and begins at the crossroads. The track to the left is called Le Chemin des Soudards (in Jersey *soudard* means a soldier and not, as in modern French, mercenary, hardened soldier or ruffian).

51

The soldiers were Les Cracots du Coin for whom the track served as a short cut to St Ouen's Church when attending militia drills there.

If you go down Le Chemin des Soudards, you will find the way barred at the head of the northern arm of Val de la Mare reservoir and you will therefore have to retrace your steps. Nevertheless a walk to the head of the reservoir is highly recommended.

The walk continues along Le Mont Rossignol where, on the left, about 150 yards beyond Le Chemin des Soudards there is a sign pointing to 'Maison de l'Amiral'. This is now only a site, the ruins of the house having been cannibalized by a builder. 'L'Amiral' is said to be Admiral Philip Carteret (Philippe de Carteret), an 18th-century navigator who discovered Pitcairn Island, gave his name to one of the Solomon Archipelago and contributed considerably to contemporary geographical knowledge.

Now take the first turning to the right into La Rue de la Campagne. *Campagne* means open country and this is just what it is. Here a survival of an ancient form of farming is to be found. Groups of strips of land separated by grass banks can clearly be seen, with remnants of the cross-strips or headlands on which ploughs were turned. The groups are called *riages*, or officially *réages*, the strips *camps*, and the cross-strips *vaindifs*. The holder of the *vaindif* could only plough when the ploughing of the *camps* was completed and then he had to leave a three-foot-wide *vaindivage* for access to the *camps*.

La Rue de la Campagne emerges at the head of Le Mont Mathieu. Here turn to the right and proceed through La Ville de l'Eglise to St Ouen's Church.

4 miles (6.4 km)

Start: St Lawrence's Parish hall; SO Map ref. 626 519
Part of the way may be very muddy

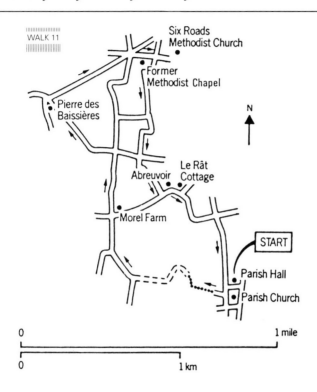

Fifty years ago when the Militia was an active force, St Lawrence was unique among Jersey parishes, for within a very small area there was a community centre more complete than in any other parish—church, parish hall, school, arsenal, shop and inn. The shop is now closed and the arsenal has been converted into dwellings, but the grounds being fortunately free from additional dwellings, the buildings and their surroundings remain a fair representative of the Island's country arsenals.

There is parking space around the parish hall, and by kind permission of the Constable, walkers may leave their cars there.

Set off down the road between the parish hall and the churchyard in the direction away from the main road and turn left at the end. Just before a house on the right (Abbey Gate) turn right into a field track and continue along the footpath which lies directly ahead. The path descends into a valley where it becomes a track much used by cattle. Having crossed the valley floor, it turns to the left and runs along the other side of the valley, rising as it goes. It then takes a turn to the right, where there is a magnificent view over heavily wooded country.

The track emerges at the side of Badier Farm, which has a double-arched entrance and enclosed courtyard, and goes straight ahead to join the highway. Shortly you arrive at a T junction with Le Chemin des Montagnes where you turn to the right. As you do so, you will see ahead a track, between two fields, said to be a *chemin de corps* (*c'min d'corps*) along which funeral processions passed on their way to St Lawrence's Church.

Le Chemin des Montagnes leads north to its junction with Les Charrières de Malorey and then assumes the name of the latter. Soon you will see Morel Farm across the field on the right. The property of the National Trust for Jersey, the farmhouse and buildings are in an excellent state of preservation and contain much of interest.

The farm stands at a crossroads where you continue straight ahead into La Rue du Rouge Cul. The house on the left some way up the road used to be Harleston House School, one of the country schools which provided a sound education in the days before the school bus and the motor car facilitated centralisation. (Harleston House is on Mont Isaac and you will be passing it later on this walk.)

On reaching a crossroads about 100 yards ahead, take the road to the left which will lead you to St Matthew's Roman Catholic Church. As you emerge at the junction with three other roads, you will see opposite you a large building which was formerly a convent school. The road from which you have come and the road on the left make a hairpin bend, and at the peak of the bend there is a weathered red granite boulder, a rough cube with sides measuring between 24 and 30 inches, called La Pierre des Baissières or La Pierre des Bessières. It has five cup marks of stone age significance. Some say that it served as the base of a wayside cross, but nothing definite is known about it.

Now turn to the right into La Longue Rue, and in due course you will arrive at Six Rues (Six Roads). Take the second road on your right and soon you will pass a large building on your right, a former Methodist chapel. The second to be built in Jersey, it dates from 1811.

Turn right into a lane, La Rue d'Avranches. Down this lane you will have the opportunity of seeing the south gable of the former Methodist chapel which is literally filled with windows. Further on there is a public pump set on a platform which, cement-covered as it is, must be the most unattractive public pump in Jersey.

On arriving at a road junction, continue ahead into a narrow lane which ends at a crossroads, and here go ahead into Mont Isaac. This is the district of La Ville au Veslet where there are houses worth noticing, particularly an L-shaped one at the top of the hill and Harleston House in the angle below. At the foot of the hill you will join La Rue de la Fontaine St Martin where, taking the road downhill to the left, you will find an *abreuvoir* on the left of the road. This is a rectangular stone trough into which the valley stream pours to pass back through the roadside wall and continue within the wall until it crosses the road.

Further down the road is the well, La Fontaine de St Martin, which gives the road its name. It lies at the foot of a wooded slope belonging to the National Trust for Jersey, a body which also owns the cottage across the road on the left, Le Rât Cottage, and the meadow between the cottage and the *abreuvoir*.

Go up the hill leading off to the right and at the crossroads turn right into the road which will lead you back to your starting place.

3 ³/₄ miles (6 km)

Start: Rue de Brabant, Trinity; SO Map ref. 656 527
Part of the way may be muddy

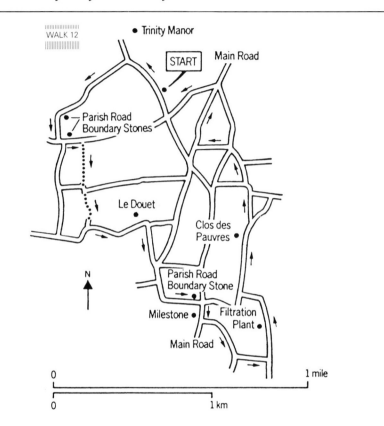

The first milestone on Trinity Hill faces the top of the old hill;
the second is on the left of the road about 40 yards before
Beechfield Lane. Half a mile further on, the road forks, and the
left fork, La Rue des Ifs, passes through La Croix. At the
crossroads, it continues as La Rue de Brabant.

Park your car in La Rue de Brabant and set out northwards. The garden of Brabant was savaged by the October 1987 hurricane. The tops of the limes were blown off; the trunks are now busily making new heads. You will shortly come to a lodge on the right of the road at the entrance to Trinity Manor, a glimpse of which is to be obtained through the trees.

About 100 yards beyond the entrance to the Manor, turn left into a lane which crosses a shallow valley, rises and winds, and then leaves the parish of Trinity for the parish of St John. The boundary is indicated by the very humblest of parish road boundary stones which leans precariously against the wall on the left of the road. The stone is of cement, about 18 inches high, and bears the letters St J. Note the change of texture of the road surface where the duty to maintain the road passes from one parish to the other.

The lane turns to the left and ends at a T junction. Turning left at the junction you will almost immediately re-enter the parish of Trinity, and here you will find the most magnificent of all the parish road boundary stones. Continue ahead (eastwards) for about 150 yards until you reach a Jersey Electricity Co transformer on the right of the road. The walk continues along the path at its side. The path descends and at the foot of the slope becomes confused with the bed of a brook, a condition which makes its viability variable.

The path emerges onto a road, and the walk continues directly ahead along another path. This path, towards its end, swings to the left and emerges on to a narrow lane with a tarmac surface where you have to turn to the right. At the end of the lane, turn to the left.

If you find the paths too muddy, you can avoid them by going down the road opposite the St John/Trinity parish road boundary stone, taking the second turning to the left and following the road round to the exit from the second path where you continue ahead.

The road crosses a valley and takes a turn to the right at the entrance to Le Douet Farm. After it has done so, continue ahead for a little over a quarter of a mile to where the road takes a turn to the left to arrive at a crossroads. At the foot of the bank on the left of the road from which you are emerging there is a parish road boundary stone bearing the initials CR, denoting the Trinity Vingtaine de la Croiserie.

Now turn to the right. In about 100 to 150 yards there is a two-mile stone set into the wall on the right, a companion to the four-mile stone to be seen on Walk 6. Very shortly turn left into Beechfield Lane which curves to the right and then slopes downhill. Take the first turning to the left into a narrow lane which ends at La Rue de la Roulerie, a T junction, where you turn to the left. The buildings on the left which you will soon be passing house the Augrès Filtration Plant of the Jersey New Waterworks Company.

Take the first turning to the left, and where the lane ends at a T junction opposite a house formerly, and aptly, named East View (whose cast iron railings merit your notice) turn to the right.

A fine view over the main valley of the Grands Vaux now opens up to the right. The field bounded by a random stone wall some way ahead on the left is, as is shown by the stone built into the wall, a *Clos des Pauvres* of the parish of Trinity, shared between the *Don Jeanne Gruchy* and the *Charité*, that is to say, the assets devoted to the maintenance of the native poor. The areas v.9.7.0. and v.2.3.0. engraved on the stone are Jersey land measure made up of vergees, perches and feet, a total of 11 $1/4$ vergees or five acres, an acre being equivalent to 2 $1/4$ vergees. (see p. 60).

DON GRUCHY STONE, TRINITY

About 100 yards beyond the Clos des Pauvres, gateposts on the same side of the road bear the initials JGC and JRM.

In another 250 yards the road takes a turn to the left, and almost immediately there is a road on the right along which the walk continues. Where it emerges onto the main road, cross into the lane opposite, and where that lane ends at a T junction, turn to the right.

Extensive views over the high lands on either side of the Grands Vaux open up once more and, at the end of the lane, the white steeple of Trinity Church is to be seen over the trees to the north. Turn to the left. The road leads to a crossroads where, by turning to the right, you will reach your starting point. While on your way notice on the left of the road, at the farmyard entrance of Le Carrefour, a mounting block with steps on either side which has been cannibalized by the removal of some of the steps.

Walk 13   **From Maufant into Trinity**
2 ³/₄ and 4 ¹/₂ miles (4.4 and 7.2 km)

Start: La Fosse à l'Écrivain; SO Map ref. 675 512
There are two moderately steep hills on the long route

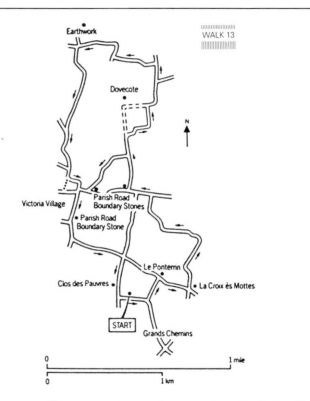

The next two walks start from the road called La Fosse à l'Écrivain, which joins the St Martin's Main Road at Grands Chemins, north of Five Oaks. La Fosse à l'Écrivain is the third turning to the left after leaving Five Oaks in the direction of St Martin's Church.

From Grands Chemins, La Fosse à l'Écrivain leads into a shallow valley and, after curving to the left out of the valley,

62

passes a lane on the right and becomes straight and level for about 200 yards. This part of the road should provide a suitable parking place.

Return towards Grands Chemins on foot and take the first turning to the left into a lane which will bring you to Le Ponterrin, a property comprising two houses of considerable age, interest and attraction. The double archway which faces you when you reach the end of the lane is unusual, as the smaller arch has been converted into a window.

The walk continues to the right which gives you the opportunity of seeing the whole of the frontage of the house on the far side of the yard. At the side of the house fronting the road are a couple of pigsties.

The road rises to a crossroads, La Croix ès Mottes. Turn to the left into La Rue du Vieux Ménage, and as you enter it, observe the wall on the right which is built of such a wide variety of stone that there can be few Jersey quarries unrepresented. Note also the mortar, the lime of which is derived from calcined sea shells.

One is now approaching the heart of Maufant. The valley is shallow enough, and further north, as the land flattens out, water tends to lie after heavy rain. Thus, in days when adequate drainage was lacking, one might have found in this area the *mal fange* (evil mire) that gave rise to the name Maufant.

In due course, the lane curves to the left and soon you will come to the entrance to the property on the left of the road, at the left of which is a gatepost bearing the initials IPD and MBT and the date 1750. Almost immediately the view opens up to the right (north) showing the top of a silo in the near distance. The lane winds again, straightens out, and then passes through an S bend. On the farm to the left of the head of the lane may be seen a building designed expressly to house racing pigeons. It is, however, no longer in use for this purpose.

At the head of the lane there is a T junction. Here turn to the left, passing behind the farm with the pigeon lofts. Take the first turning to the right, noting in the hedge on the left of the road a parish road boundary stone between the parishes of St Saviour and Trinity, denoted by the marks 'S'S' and 'TN'' on the stone.

At the next road junction you have the option of a long route or a short one.

ENTRANCE GATEWAY NEAR DIÉLAMENT MANOR

Long route Continue ahead. In about 100 yards, on the left of the road, are the derelict remains of what is said to have been the entrance to Diélament Manor. An early 19th-century engraving shows the entrance and a long and lofty avenue of beech trees, but all the trees have gone, no trace of the avenue can be seen, and there remains only a sad, grand gateway, now no more than an entrance to a field.

A little further on, the road turns to the right. A track ahead leads to the Diélament Manor House of the present time which stands beyond the head of the track, with a *colombier* (dovecote) at its side, stemming from the time when the Lord of the Manor enjoyed the sole right to keep pigeons.

The road continues by right-angled turns and arrives at a small group of houses. Beyond them, take the first turning to the left into a winding lane which leads down into a valley on the right of which are the grounds of the Zoo at Augrès Manor.

The lane mounts and at the top of the rise is a farm, Les Câteaux. This takes its name from the earthwork nearby on the right-hand side of the lane branching off to the north (right). It is the remains of a medieval bank and ditch enclosure for the protection of people and their animals when the Island was raided. At the left of the entrance to the farm is a mounting block with steps on either side and above it a stone bowl which must surely have served originally as a holy water stoup in a church.

Turn left opposite the farm entrance into a lane which shortly leads downhill, crosses a valley, and mounts to enter La Boucterie (Victoria Village) where the short route comes in from the left.

Short route At the parting of the routes, take the road on the left. A little way down on the right, there is a shapely house well worth noticing, with elaborate decorative woodwork on its dormer windows. The lane ends at a T junction where, on the left corner at the foot of the bank, there is a parish road boundary stone with the initials TN^t on one face and the initials S'S on another. The road to the left as far as you can see it, and beyond, is maintained by St Saviour, but the land on both sides is in Trinity.

Turn right at the T junction to enter the northern end of La Boucterie (Victoria Village) where the long route is joined.

The routes reunited Continue southwards through the village. The farm on the left a little way down the road suffered bomb damage during the Second World War, slight indications of which are visible. The right-hand gatepost bears the initials IAL.

The last house in the village on the left of the road is the first house in St Saviour, but the parish road boundary stone is further on, opposite the appropriately named house, La Frontière, the last house in Trinity. The boundary stone is more elaborate than most, and second only to that between St John's and Trinity which is to be seen on Walk 12.

Continue ahead and take the first turning to the left opposite the house whose fine wrought ironwork decorating the entrance merits appreciation. Formerly bordering the yard of St Thomas's Roman Catholic Church in Val Plaisant, St Helier, it was brought here in 1976, and though heavily damaged by the fall of enormous evergreen oaks in the 1987 hurricane it should be restored by the time this is in print.

On arriving at the crossroads, turn right. Some way down the road, on the right-hand side, is the *Clos des Pauvres* of the parish of St Saviour, bought with the parish's share of the bequest of Miss Jeanne Gruchy.

Just beyond the field, the road to the left is your starting place. As you turn the corner, observe the house on the right, Château Clairval, recently rebuilt in the style of the original, a nice example of Victoriana.

Walk 14
3³/₄ miles (6 km)

From Maufant into St Martin's

Start: La Fosse à l'Écrivain; SO Map ref. 675 512 (see Walk 13)

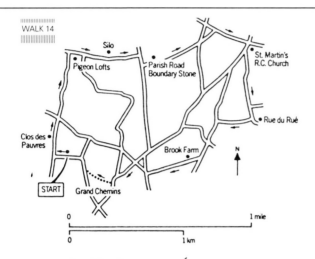

At the western end of La Fosse à l'Écrivain is Château Clairval, easily recognizable because of its crenellations. Here, at a T junction, turn right. A little way up the road you will come to the *Clos des Pauvres* of the parish of St Saviour, marked by a stone which commemorates Miss Jeanne Gruchy, the donor of the funds with which it was bought.

At the next crossroads, go ahead into La Rue de la Guilleaumerie, and in about 250 yards you will see on the right of the road a house which stood derelict for very many years and which was restored in 1975-6. Observe, in the wall bordering the road, a blocked-up doorway spanned by a lintel bearing the date 1734 and the initials EDH and SN on either side of a single heart.

The road now enters an S bend at the end of which a farm comes into view on the right of the road with, on its far side, a concrete building of unusual appearance. It was built specifically to house racing pigeons, but is no longer used for that purpose.

The farm stands at a T junction with the house 'La Guilleaumerie' on the other corner. Turn right into La Rue du Pont, and in about 40 yards, as you near a field entrance, you will see the steeple of St Martin's Church on the skyline somewhat to the left ahead.

You next come to a T junction with the Maufant road. Turn to the right and then turn left into La Rue du Sacrement. As the road turns to the right, a change in the texture of the road surface is to be seen. The reason for the change will be found in the bank on the left where there is a parish road boundary stone bearing the letters S'S and SM on adjoining faces. This stone between St Saviour's and St Martin's has been badly battered and appears to be of a very early date.

The road descends gently into a shallow valley, passing on the way the entrance to a farm, La Chasse, on the left of the road with a gatepost bearing the initials PBT and RDP, the date 1823 and interlocking hearts.

Emerging from the road which, on entering St Martin's, has taken the name of La Rue des Cabarettes, cross into La Rue du Carrefour. Where this is joined by another road, follow it to the right. St Martin's Church is once more in view, now at no great distance. In due course, you will come to St Martin's main road, on the far side of which is St Martin's Roman Catholic Church.

Turn right down the main road and very shortly enter La Route des Buttes on the left. The road's name changes at the junction on the left with La Rue des Fontaines (which you ignore) and becomes La Rue du Rué.

Take the first turning to the right into La Rue de Benjamin from which you will see the *rué* or brook in the valley on the left. At the T junction at the end of La Rue de Benjamin, turn to the left, and on reaching another T junction, turn left again. The four round granite pillars at the back of the house (now called Le Picachon) on the left of the road used to stand in the Public Markets in St Helier.

Now turn right into La Route du Champ Colin which takes a turn to the left and then rises by a gentle slope at the top of which a lane comes in on the right. This is La Rue du Sergent or Brook Farm Lane, and the walk continues along it, passing on the way Brook Farm and a large housing estate built in 1976/7. Away on the left is the wooded mound of La Hougue Bie.

The lane emerges on La Rue du Trot at a T junction. Turn to the right and where the road forks not far ahead take the left fork. This will bring you to St Martin's main road where you turn to the left.

Some way down, the road passes through an S bend and a by-road comes in on the right, and beyond it there is a house with a very steeply pitched roof. This was built not long after the demise of the Jersey Eastern Railway and incorporated several of the company's passenger carriages. The carriages were short by modern standards; an example is to be seen at La Hougue Bie. They have now been removed, but there are some who still refer to it as the 'railway carriage house'.

Where the road leaves the S bend, there is a track on the right along which the walk continues. The first part passes in front of a row of houses and has a tarmac surface. It continues along the side of a field and then descends between high hedges into La Fosse à l'Écrivain. Turn to the right and you will soon be back at your starting place.

Walk 15

North of St Martin's Public Hall

3 miles (4.8 km)

Start: St Martin's Public Hall; SO Map ref. 690 525

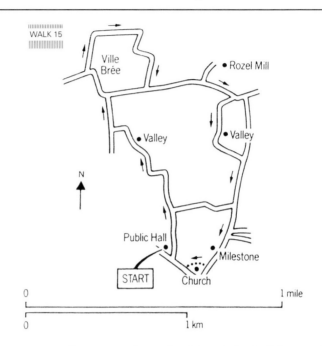

The next two walks start from St Martin's Public Hall on the road to Trinity to the west of St Martin's Church. There is a small car park in front of the hall where, by kind permission of the Constable, walkers may leave their cars.

Set off in a northerly direction down La Rue des Raisies on the east side of the Public Hall. Eventually the road turns to the left, and after a turn to the right, descends into a valley and crosses it, emerging at a T junction on to a main road.

At this point, turn to the right, and as you pass up the road, take a look at La Franchise Farm across the field on the left, a house of double depth which, unusually, has full sized windows set into its gable end.

You will come to another T junction at the top of the road, and here turn to the left. The road almost immediately takes a turn to the right, and some way further on, a turn to the left. Just after the latter turn there is a lane, La Rue de la Ville Brée, leading off to the right.

Where the lane turns to the right at its foot, it becomes La Rue du Rât. Some way along, views of the sea open up with the Dirouilles to the north, and continuing from their eastern end, the Ecréhos. The road now runs downhill to a corner where it turns to the right and then proceeds uphill. Next comes a turn to the left and the Dirouilles and the Ecréhos are again to be seen. The lane then turns to the right and emerges on to the main road at a T junction. On its final length, the name of the lane is La Rue des Huriaux.

At this point, turn left. On the left of the road stands Rozel Mill which shows clear indications of fortification by the Germans during the Occupation. Just after you have passed the entrance to the lane which leads to the mill, a fine view to the south opens up on the right of the road.

The road now curves gently to the right and very soon a lane on the right is reached. The lane and the road down which you have come make a hairpin bend, and it is down this lane that the walk continues. After passing a few houses on the left, the lane turns to the left and goes steeply downhill. At the first entrance to the farm half way down the hill, the left-hand gatepost bears the initials FAM and DLS and the date 1623. Clumps of bamboos in the valley provide an oriental touch and the lane then rises to meet the road between Rozel Bay and St Martin's Church. Turn right towards the church. The road proceeds uphill, and just before it begins to descend notice the blacksmith's forge on the left of the road. Where the road curves to the right on its ascent towards the church, note also the four-mile stone set into the wall on the right.

Turn into the churchyard when you reach it, passing behind the church and noting its blocked up windows and heavily buttressed north walls. On leaving the churchyard, go ahead along the granite paved pedestrian way which will bring you to the road leading to the Public Hall.

Start: St Martin's Hall; SO Map ref. 690 525 (see Walk 15)

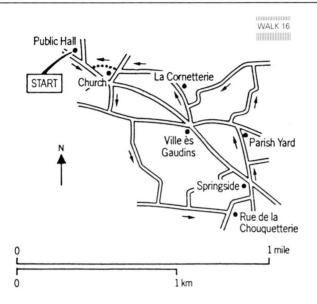

Set off towards the church and on reaching it, go down La Rue de Payn which joins the main road opposite the south side of the churchyard. On arriving at a T junction, turn left and then take the first turning to the right into La Rue de l'Orme. The cider apple trees growing on a bank between fields to the right of the road where it turns to the left were possibly planted there to avoid payment of tithes to the Rector of St Martin. It is said that tithes on apples were due only on those grown in fields and thus those grown on boundary banks were exempt.

Where the road ends at a T junction, turn left and continue to the next T junction, passing on the way La Beuvelande camping site on the right and shortly afterwards, on the left, a lane which will make a pleasant detour if you pass this way on a subsequent occasion.

La Rue de la Chouquetterie is reached at the T junction, and here turn left. The road soon takes a turn to the right and, after mounting a minor slope on each side of which there is a round-arched doorway worthy of your attention, arrives at a T junction where you find that you are emerging, not from La Rue de la Chouquetterie, but from La Rue du Bouillon. At this junction, turn to the left and you will shortly come to the main road between St Martin's Church and Gorey, with the house Springside on your left.

Go ahead at this point and in due course you will arrive at St Martin's Parish Yard, flanked by a pillar bearing the date 1888, on the right of the road, and beyond it the road between St Martin's Church and St Catherine's Bay.

Turn left up the road and very shortly turn right into La Verte Rue, a name which attaches to many roads in Jersey, there being also a Green Road and a Green Street. After a turn to the right and just before a twist to the left, look in at a field entrance for a fine view over the valley through which St Catherine's Hill descends, with St Catherine's Breakwater appearing to cross most of the mouth of the bay. St Catherine's Bay remains visible as, after a turn to the right and a turn to the left, you pass down the lane which ends at a T junction. Now turn to the left and keep ahead for quite a distance. When the lane turns to the left, observe the inscription, dated 1821, on the sill of the window above the front door of the house on the right, Le Fleurion. It consists of the initials GLSL and FMSV linked by an ampersand (&) instead of the customary heart or interlocking hearts.

The lane soon turns to the right and ends when it shows its name to be La Rue de la Forge. The walk continues to the right, but if you wish to see a few items of interest, turn left to the nearby crossroads at La Ville ès Gaudins. Facing you as you arrive at the crossroads is a granite entrance doorway, bearing the name 'La Frênaie' (the Ash Grove) and the date 1626. The date is misleading, for the doorway was built at the turn of the century by Thomas William Messervy, Constable of St Martin from 1865 to 1877. The carving is distinctly modern and the purpose of the building is anybody's guess, because prior to the recently built houses behind it—the nearest of which has adopted the name on the doorway—the erection gave entrance only to a large field. To your right, at the foot of the road from St Martin's Church, is Les Alpes, where Mr Messervy lived and indulged his architectural fancies. More mundane are the granite trough and pump at the road junction to your right. This facility, apparently, is not available to the public but only to the houses of the successors of those who established it.

Now turn back to the lane by which you have come and continue ahead (as if you had turned to the right on emerging from La Rue de la Forge). A gentle slope downhill brings you to a field entrance at the side of which there is a large round rough-hewn granite column about seven feet high. It stands on the lands of La Cornetterie, the house further up the road, which at one time also belonged to Mr Messervy. It was probably he who erected the column.

At the foot of the field path is a *lavoir* (*douet à laver*) called Le Douet de Fleury fed by a brook (*douet*) which, joined by other brooks, finds its way into the sea through the shingle below the White Tower in St Catherine's Bay. The *lavoir* has on either side of its entrance granite pillars bearing the date 1832 and the initials of the owners of houses in the vicinity who were entitled to use it for washing their household linen.

The walk continues past La Cornetterie, the name of which, together with a couple of cornets, appears on an elegant granite tablet set into the side of the house. The granite pillars on either side of the garden entrance, and two more supporting the roof of the lean-to behind the house, clearly come from the old Public markets of St Helier. Similar pillars are to be seen on Walks 14 and 19.

Further on the road bears to the left, and on the right is Bandinel Farm which takes its name from the Bandinel family, originally Bandinelli, of Italian origin, a family which provided Jersey with its first Anglican Dean.

You are now in La Chasse ès Demoiselles which leads directly to St Martin's Church. Continue into the churchyard and pass to the north of the church, for here you will see the great number of buttresses which have had to be built to support the north walls—one of them across a window opening—and at the western end, so many as to leave room only for a lancet and a two-light window.

On leaving the churchyard, continue ahead along the granite-paved pathway to the public road and there turn right to reach the Public Hall.

Walk 17

Inland from St Catherine's

3 ½ miles (5.6km)

Start: St Catherine's cross-roads; SO Map ref. 707 523
Part of the way may be extremely muddy

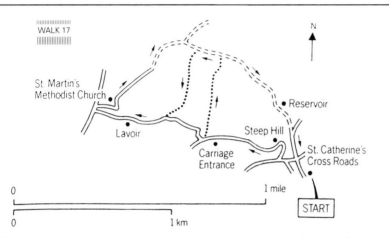

Park your car in the road leading from Archirondel to St Catherine's crossroads. At the crossroads, turn left up St Catherine's Hill and take the first turning to the right up a road which comes in on a hairpin bend. Notice the fountain set into the wall on the left—a granite trough of quite the smallest size, backed by a scooped-out granite pillar about three and a half feet high, clearly a spout designed for funnelling water into or over something. This may have come from the nearby Moulin de la Perrelle at the foot of the valley down which this walk ends. Neither the pillar nor the glazed garden tile cemented to its base now serve anything other than a decorative purpose.

Some way up the hill, where the road curves to the right, pause to admire the view over St Catherine's Bay, one which would have been very different if the Admiralty's project for building a harbour there had been completed. As it is, the abandonment of the project led to the transfer to the States of Jersey of a great area of land extending from the track leading down to the beach at Archirondel as far as the slipway in Fliquet Bay 'to be held by them in trust for the public service of the Island'.

ST. CATHERINE'S BREAKWATER

Observe the two round granite stones with broad arrows incised on their top surfaces on either side of the entrance to a grassy track on the left of the hill, and a third stone 20 to 30 feet down the track. These stones are exceptional, as boundary stones are normally square in shape; the broad arrow is a distinguishing mark for British Government property.

Towards the top of the hill, somewhat splendid carriage and pedestrian entrances with round pillars formed of rectangular rough-faced granite blocks, surmounted by an arrangement of sharp-edged stones to give the effect of flaming torches, are to be seen on the near side of the farmhouse on the left. Beyond lies an open field and it seems reasonable to assume that the entrance was intended for a residence which was never built.

FLAMBOYANT GATEPOSTS AT ST. CATHERINE'S

Where shortly afterwards the road curves to the left, you will come to a track on the right of the road bordered on either side by hedge-topped earth banks. Go down the track, and as you proceed along it, you will have fine views over the valley below, with Rozel Manor on its far side. At the end of the track, the way ceases to be clearly defined, but you should have no difficulty in descending the wooded hillside at the foot of which a track passes up the valley.

On the far side of the track is a meadow forming part of the grounds of Rozel Manor; on the near side (where you are) is La Grande Commune du Fief de la Reine en St Martin.

Turn to the left up the track, and where a tributary valley comes in on the left, go up it following the track which runs

79

along its side. There is a stream on the right and in due course the track crosses it and continues along the other side of the valley, coming to an end in a small meadow with a lane beyond.

LAVOIR AT ST. MARTIN'S

On reaching the lane, turn to the right. Soon you will come to a granite trough on the left, behind which there is a tall narrow granite pillar inscribed with sets of initials, and the date 1846. The trough is a *lavoir* and *abreuvoir* established by those whose initials are inscribed on the pillar. The water for the trough is supplied by a pipe from a spring called La Fontaine de Gallie, a form of supply which is unusual. Most *lavoirs* are built on a watercourse (*douet*) and hence the derivation of the description of them as *douets à laver* or *dous à laver.* The right to use the trough attaches to houses in the vicinity, subject however to 48 hours' previous notice being given. The stonework at the side was possibly designed to serve for beating the linen and stacking it after washing, as use of the meadow for drying it was forbidden. The choice of the initials for designating the names follows the usual pattern— Philippe VarDon, Nicolas ReNouf, Abraham Le HuQuet etc.— but the last is not easy, for CP designates La Chapelle Méthodiste de St Martin which you will be passing as you continue on your way. Hinge pivots set into the walls on either side of the *lavoir* indicate that it once had doors, no doubt to prevent its unauthorized use.

Further up the lane on the right is a cottage called 'La Carrière' (The Quarry), and at its side the quarry from which stone for the cottage appears to have been taken. This is an example of the bygone practice of going the shortest possible distance for building stone and, if necessary, opening a quarry expressly for the purpose, a quarry which might never be used again.

When the lane comes to an end, take the hairpin bend to the right into another lane which rises and soon passes St Martin's Methodist church—the ChaPelle of the *lavoir*. Some way ahead, the lane turns left, loses its tarmac surface, and becomes a track which descends into a wooded valley. At the foot of the descent the track divides, one branch going uphill to the left. Do not take the left-hand branch, but go straight ahead down the valley, passing on the way the mouth of the tributary valley through which you passed earlier in the walk and the wooded hillside which you descended. On your way you will have to pass over a small outcrop of rock, and when you come to a small flat area where the path is ill-defined, bear left to cross the stream (which you may have to jump, though it's not very wide). The path curves and brings you back to the stream which here is crossed by stepping stones. It now broadens to become a track, passes a reservoir created by the Germans during the Occupation and emerges onto the public highway where Le Moulin de la Perrelle is to be seen at the foot of the hill on the left. The place from which you started this walk lies ahead.

Walk 18

2 ¹/₂ miles (4 km)

Faldouet

Start: East of the top of Gorey Hill; SO Map ref. 711 505

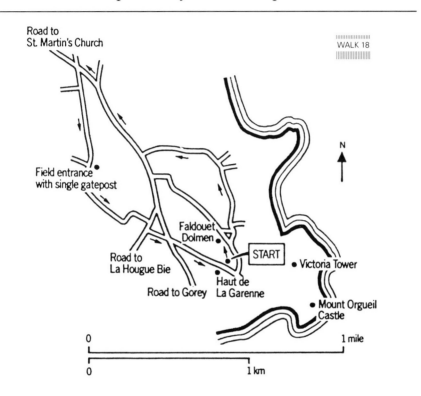

Make for La Rue de la Pouclée et des Quatre Chemins, which is the first turning to the right as the road levels out at the top of Gorey Hill.

The road widens towards its far end and there should be no objection to your car being parked here. The institution to the right of the road is Haut de la Garenne, formerly the Jersey Home for Boys, with which the Jersey Female Orphans' home was combined in 1961. It may be familiar to viewers of

'Bergerac' as the original of the mythical 'Bureau des Etrangers'. The site is at present (1992) the subject of development plans.

The walk begins along the lane to the left, but first go straight ahead and you will shortly find yourself above Mont Orgueil Castle and Gorey Harbour. Note the round turrets at the top of the Castle, built by the Germans during the Occupation and thereby extending the fortification of the headland from medieval times to the present day. To the right is Grouville Bay, and beyond it St Clement's Bay, meeting at La Rocque Point, the south-east corner of Jersey, with Seymour Tower offshore and Icho Tower in St Clement's Bay.

Follow the lane where it curves to the left. The buildings on the right are the Old Cadet House, so called because they used to house a Royal Naval Training School. Where the lane divides, take the left fork and in 15 yards you will come to a path lined with thorn hedges which will lead you to Faldouet Dolmen, the property of the Société Jersiaise and open to view without charge. Faldouet Dolmen (La Pouquelaye de Faldouet) is a megalithic passage grave which, so far as Jersey structures of this period are concerned, is second only to La Hougue Bie. It is generally agreed that it was originally covered with a mound, much of which remained until the middle of the 19th century. The axis of the structure runs almost due east and west and the weight of the huge capstone of the western chamber is estimated to be between 23 and 24 tons.

As you come back along the path, you will see away ahead, and slightly to the right, Victoria Tower, a martello tower which has been adapted for use as the Victoria College Observatory.

The left and right forks just before the Dolmen form two sides of a triangle, so take either route and pick up the continuation of the right fork from which you will be able to see down into Anne Port, with, on the right-hand side, Jeffrey's Leap, the rock from which the legendary Mont Orgueil Castle prisoner bearing that name is said to have leaped to his death.

Some distance along, the lane curves to the left with two turnings off to the right. Ignore these (the first leads down to Anne Port and the second to Archirondel) and follow the curve. The lane rises, then falls, and then rises to emerge on the road between Faldouet and Gorey, showing its name to be La Rue de Guilleaume et d'Anneville.

Now turn to the right and in about half a mile take the first turning to the left into La Rue des Alleurs. The name *Les Alleurs* is to be found in many parts of Jersey. It is probably the same as *Les Alleus*, which dates from feudal times when land was normally held from an over-lord, subject to the payment of dues and the performance of services. *Alleu* is equivalent to *allodium*, which means land held free from all dues and services, such as would be the case with land belonging to the church.

Keep ahead down La Rue des Alleurs, passing two lanes on your right, and at the second, La Rue du Ministre, look southwards where Grouville Mill is to be seen in the far distance, remote on the skyline. Its sails had long since been removed when the Germans, during the Occupation, made their replacement impossible by converting the mill into an observation post and reconstructing the top in concrete.

The field entrance opposite the turn into La Rue du Ministre displays a sign of the times. One gatepost is standing and the other is missing, its removal having been made necessary to allow the access of modern agricultural machinery. You will see two more field entrances which have been similarly treated as you proceed on your way, and many more are to be seen in other parts of the Island.

Continue ahead. The lane curves and turns, and as you near its end, observe the house across the field on the right, for there is comparative rarity at the back—a round tower which accommodates a spiral stone staircase.

The lane (which, in its course, has changed its name to La Chasse Mallet) emerges at a T junction onto the road between Faldouet and La Hougue Bie. At this point, turn to the right, and very shortly afterwards turn left. The road rises and crosses the road between Faldouet and Gorey to enter La Rue de la Pouclée et des Quatre Chemins where this walk started.

On your way towards Haut de la Garenne, and just before you reach it, look to the right for another view of the Bays of Grouville and St Clement, with La Rocque Point in between, and this time with the spire of Gorey Church in the foreground.

Start: La Rue du Trot; SO Map ref. 683 505

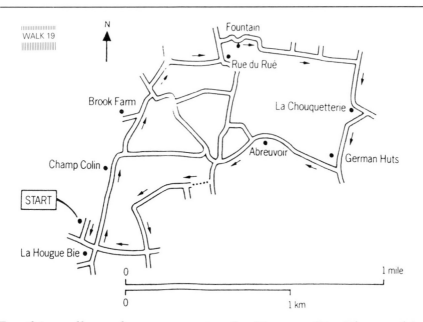

For this walk, park your car near La Hougue Bie. The road in front of the entrance is suitable, but as coaches bringing visitors normally park there, you may find it preferable (depending on the time of day and the period of the year) to park your car in La Rue du Trot (B46), the road leading to Maufant crossroads and Trinity.

Set off down La Route du Champ Colin which is the lane running north from the point where the Prince's Tower Road from Five Oaks turns east towards Gorey.

On a clear day, the hills above Gorey are visible to the east, with the sea and the French coast beyond. About 200 yards down the lane you will come to a series of granite posts lining

WIND PUMP NEAR LA HOUGUE BIE

the field on the left. Some of the posts have flat iron staples set into their tops and others are surmounted by short iron rods equipped with washers and fasteners. Both the staples and rods are designed to secure wooden rails running from one post to the other. This device is called *les barres*, a form of post and rail fencing.

Beyond the farmhouse Champ Colin on the left, La Route du Champ Colin turns to the right and in about ten yards turns to the left at its junction with La Rue de Neuilly. Do not go down La Rue de Neuilly but follow La Route du Champ Colin to the left. Over the field in front is a farm house (with three

..indows on the first storey) called Brook Farm, taking its name from the brook which rises in the neighbourhood. This brook eventually joins with others to form the main brook of Queen's Valley, all of them, after heavy rains in the early part of 1978, having combined to cause serious flooding in Gorey Village.

The lane twists and soon joins a lane leading to Brook Farm. Go straight ahead at this point. After 100 yards or so, the lane turns to the right and shortly comes to an end. In front is a house now called Le Picachon, which means a small triangular plot of land. Turn left, and on passing the back of the house, observe the four round granite pillars which used to stand in the Public Markets in St Helier. Similar pillars are to be seen on Walk 16.

A little further on, take the lane to the right and on its left you will see the brook which, at this point, divides the parish of St Martin from the parish of St Saviour. The brook used to run in an open channel on the left of the road, but has now been culverted. Soon you will reach a farm called Les Prés on the right of the road, and beyond it, La Rue de Benjamin. The brook here crosses under the road (ceasing its function as a divider of parishes) and emerges to pass eastwards through the meadows which give Les Prés its name.

Turning right into, and proceeding along, La Rue de Benjamin, one arrives in due course at La Rue du Rué. Here turn left, and a little over 100 yards up the lane, turn right into La Rue des Fontaines. The lane dips as it twists and turns and at the foot of the dip is a fountain of clear water at road surface level.

Now come two interesting examples of marriage stones. The first is on the house on the left of the road just beyond the fountain, where the incised inscription on the stone shows the year 1732 and the initials ILM and MBT separated by a single dot. The second example is not far ahead.

At some point the lane becomes la Rue de Beuvelande, possibly where it turns to the left on reaching high ground. At this turn one can see La Hougue Bie on the southern horizon. Nearby trees obscure the view, but the mound is identifiable by the high outhouses to its right. On a clear day, the sea to the south of the Island is also visible.

Just beyond the turn is a farm called Beauchamp on the left of the lane. There is a marriage stone of later date, 1753, above the main door of the house, which has a single heart separating the initials EGD and FNC. The inscription here is in raised letters and figures.

Continuing along the lane you will pass La Beuvelande camping site on your right and reach La Rue de la Chouquetterie at a T junction where the walk continues to the right. Some way ahead where the lane curves to the left, St Saviour's Hospital, somewhat obscured by new extensions, is to be seen across the valley ahead. Passing the house La Chouquetterie on your right, follow the road downhill by a hairpin bend into the valley.

At the bottom of the hill, on the right of the road, stand two wooden huts, relics of the German Occupation. Shortly afterwards, turn right into La Rue du Côtil which lies in the parish of St Saviour. The road changes its name to La Rue St Julien opposite the farm Le Côtil at the point where the parish of St Martin is re-entered. The dividing line between the parishes is clearly shown on the road surface, for this is a by-road maintained at parish expense. About 20 yards before the parish boundary, across the field to the left is a stone well-head, and within St Martin's is a roadside fountain with an *abreuvoir* adjoining it. A little way beyond across the field on the left, observe a small quarry from which, as from so many small quarries which are to be found in Jersey, stone for buildings in the neighbourhood was derived.

The next road junction is with La Rue de Baudains, a hill to the right, opposite which is Valley Farm where, in the winter months, cider was made until recently using a stone crusher and wooden press.

Proceed along La Rue St Julien to a crossroads where the walk continues along the road to the left. The road rises, and part of the way up, there is a footpath on the right. Enter the footpath and go straight ahead when it comes to an end. In due course the road turns to the left and eventually emerges onto Prince's Tower Road. (The house Tower Hamlet is on your left.) Here turn right up the main road and you will soon be back at La Hougue Bie.

Walk 20   **South of La Hougue Bie**
2 ½ and 3½ miles (4 and 5.6 km)

Start: La Rue du Trot; SO Map ref 683 505 (see Walk 19)
There is one short steep hill

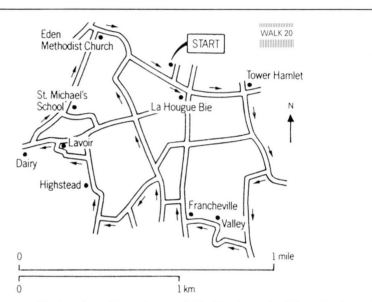

Start the walk in the direction of St Saviour's Hospital and
Gorey. Having passed the crossroads where Prince's Tower
Road meets La Rue du Trot and La Route du Champ Colin,
continue ahead to the next crossroads and there turn to the
right.

There is now a slight twist in the road where another road
comes in on the right, but continue ahead to the next right-
hand turning noticing the trees bordering the far side of the
field on your right. These line a public footpath which you
may like to walk on another occasion. On the left of the road,
there is a good view towards La Rocque Point and Seymour
Tower beyond.

The next turning to the right leads you into a lane down which you will not have gone very far before you come to something fairly rare in Jersey—a field which is level with the road, and no hedge or bank between the two.

After the lane has turned to the left, there is another lane leading off to the right. Go along it and in about 100 yards you will find a field entrance with a five-barred gate and a wonderful view over Grouville Bay. Ahead is Verclut, the hilly promontory surmounted by Grouville Mill, and at its foot on the left, the spire of Grouville Church stands out.

Further ahead the lane winds and crosses a small valley. At the top of the hill out of the valley, turn to the right and go up the road on the right side of which is the high wall of Francheville—a wall which nowadays would cost a fortune to build. When you come to the end of the wall, turn to the left into one of the rare parish roads which, though metalled, has never been given a full tarmac surface. At the end of it, turn right and proceed up the road until you reach a lane leading off to the left.

Short walk If you want a short walk, go straight on. This will bring you to Prince's Tower Road. Cross it into the road opposite which runs level for a while and then, after a gentle descent, turns to the right. Note the brook running in a narrow channel to the left of the road ahead. Open roadside brooks are now rare as, for the safety of wheeled traffic, the tendency is to cover them over.

Not far beyond the turn, set in to the wall on the right at eye level, is a marriage stone with an incised inscription showing the initials IPG and MMR separated by a single heart with the date 1805 below. About 25 yards further along is a garden gate and on its left is another marriage stone bearing the same initials, again separated by a single heart, but with the date 1754. The inscription in this case is raised. As there is a lapse of 51 years between the two dates, you have here apparent evidence of a very long marriage, but that is not the case. What you have is evidence of a coincidence—Jean Pelgué, father and son, both of whom married ladies named Marie Mourant.

Continue up the road and take the first turning to the right. It is at this point that the two routes meet.

Long walk For a longer walk, go along the lane to the left, and when the lane divides, keep to the right. Here you will have a view over St Clement's Bay, with the tops of the high-rise flats in Maupertuis Lane peeping over the hedge in the near foreground and Grève d'Azette beyond. Away to the left is the sea in Grouville Bay.

GATEPOST NEAR HIGHSTEAD, ST. SAVIOUR

When you come to a T junction, turn to the right. Up the road and on its right is a field entrance flanked by an unusual pair of gateposts, one of which bears the initials IMR in incised letters and the other the same initials and the date 1740 in raised letters and figures.

Continue along the road past Highstead and take the first turning to the left which, after turning right, left and right again, will bring you to a *lavoir* on the right of the road.

LAVOIR OFF PRINCE'S TOWER ROAD

You will now have arrived at Prince's Tower Road. Turn to the left towards Five Oaks and then take the first turning to the right (opposite the Dairy of the Jersey Milk Marketing Board) into La Rue des Friquettes and continue ahead past St Michael's Preparatory School (La Houguette) on your right. When the view opens up to the right, you will see La Hougue Bie on the skyline.

At the head of the road, on the right, is Eden Methodist Church, a plain utilitarian building relieved by an attractive doorway. Here turn right and then take the first turning to the left. Those who have chosen to take the short walk will have come along the road ahead. (If you want to see the Pelgue marriage stones, you will not have far to walk.)

The routes reunited The road into which you have turned will bring you back to La Hougue Bie. On its left is a tall three-storeyed house, La Commune, whose appearance belies its ancient origin, for within it is a single-storeyed two-roomed cottage with gables six feet thick built of rough blocks bound with clay and straw.

The first cider to be exported to Southampton came from this farm, and it is therefore not surprising to find sections of the troughs of several granite apple crushers lining the yard and the entrance to the farm on the other side of the road. There is also a fine collection of other farm granite—stack stones, troughs and a brine bath for salting meat.

As you near the top of the road, you will come to a cement-fronted house (Fairview Farm) on the left with a cement marriage stone within the console bracket over the front door, the initials J.AB and A.QR (Josué Aubin and Anne Quérée) being linked by an ampersand (&) instead of a heart or interlocking hearts. Dates on such stones can be misleading for they do not invariably indicate the date of marriage. Mr and Mrs Aubin were married 26 years before the date (1888) shown on the stone and they may well have chosen to link their names with an ampersand to indicate the passage of years since that happy event.

Observe the mounting block outside the farm on the left just before you reach La Hougue Bie.

Walk 21
2¹/₂ miles (4 km)

Les Grands Vaux

Start: Deloraine Road, St Saviour; SO Map ref. 667 502
There are two moderately steep hills

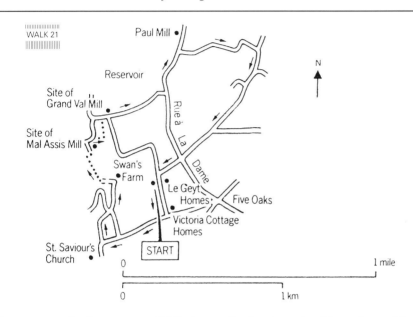

Going up St Saviour's Hill from St Saviour's Church to Five Oaks, Deloraine Road is the second turning to the left. Going down from Five Oaks to St Saviour's Church, it is the first turning to the right.

The Grainville Playing Fields are on the west side of Deloraine Road, and at their northern end is a car park where, by kind permission of the Education Committee, walkers may park their cars.

The two single-storeyed houses opposite the entrance to the car park are the Le Geyt Homes founded in memory of Queen Victoria by Miss Rosalie Anne Le Geyt, and are available for occupation, free of charge, by poor respectable persons of British nationality. Now antiquated, they are the subject of development plans (1992).

Set out towards St Saviour's Hill. To your left as you emerge from Deloraine Road are the Victoria Cottage Homes, a public foundation of 1897 to celebrate Queen Victoria's Diamond Jubilee. The original homes were opened in 1905; they are the three centre blocks and are easily recognizable because they are of granite. The buildings on either side date from 1953 and further additions have since been made.

Turn right downhill towards St Saviour's Church and if, on reaching the churchyard, you wish to see the grave of Lillie Langtry, the Jersey Lily, enter the churchyard by the gate which lies before you. Go straight ahead along the path which in due course turns to the left. The grave is on the right not far beyond the turn.

On leaving the churchyard by the same gate, turn left into Rectory Lane (or, if you continue the walk without going into the churchyard, turn right on reaching it). On the left, at the head of the lane, is St Saviour's Rectory, built in 1961 to replace the adjacent old Rectory where Lillie Langtry was born in 1853.

Follow the lane where it curves to the right and continue ahead across Langley Avenue into the lane beyond. At the foot of the lane is Swan Farm, formerly called Swan's Farm, following a practice now largely fallen into disuse of naming a farm after its owner or tenant.

The lane now turns to the left and loses its tarmac surface. In about 100 yards, turn right into a public footpath, the entrance to which is marked by a granite gatepost on the left and a low granite pillar on the right. The footpath crosses the fields and then descends into the Grands Vaux, emerging behind the

Community Centre at the upper end of the Nicholson Park housing estate.

Below the Community Centre, at the right of the foot of the track, is the site of Malassis Mill, known also at other times as Stephens's Mill, Gilley's Mill and Adams' Mill, for mills, like farms, often took the name of the occupant. The name Malassis is a very ancient one, going back to the beginning of the 14th century at least. It means badly sited, for the water necessary to work the millwheel had first to pass by the next mill up the valley, Grand Val Mill. Grand Val itself was not entirely happily placed, for water from the main valley had first to pass by Paul Mill, though it was supplemented on the way by waters from tributary valleys.

Having reached the site of Malassis Mill, your aim is now to proceed up the valley. As the layout of the land is at the present time somewhat haphazard, the best that I can do is to advise you to go ahead to the valley road and there turn to the right. Where the road turns to the left, there is a footpath on the right-hand side which, after a turn to the left, will bring you back to the valley road. The walk then continues to the right.

Very soon you will come to a derelict site on the left, that of Grand Val or Baxter's Mill. Next comes the Grands Vaux reservoir. Follow the road along its side until, near the end, you come to a lane, Les Ruettes, on the right. On the left at the foot of the hill ahead is the mill commonly called Moulin de Pol or Paul Mill which takes its name from Louys Paul alias Bertram who was miller there in the mid-16th century. The building is the sole survivor of all mill buildings in the lower part of the Grands Vaux, though the mill machinery was dismantled in 1925.

As you turn into Les Ruettes, you will see a parish road

boundary stone at the corner on the left, the initials MF and SLG denoting the St Saviour's vingtaines of Maufant and Sous l'Eglise.

In due course Les Ruettes becomes a hill, narrows, and after a turn to the left and a turn to the right, emerges opposite the former entrance of St Mannelier at the side of which there is a gatepost bearing the date 1760. Here was an ancient chapel dedicated to St Mannelier (St Magloire was a variant of the name). Here also a school for the six eastern parishes of the Island was founded in the 15th century. However, nothing of interest now remains on the site.

Turn right down the hill and you will soon come to a small building set into the bank on the right of the road and bearing the date 1771. This was originally a *chendri*, a place specially constructed to hold cinders for future use, such as for binding mortar.

On the left at the foot of the hill, beyond a field entrance and close to a flight of steps, there is a parish road boundary stone inscribed with the letters MF and PG, in this case the St Saviour's vingtaines of Maufant and Pigneaux.

ISSUE, LES CHASSES, BEL AIR LANE, ST. SAVIOUR

The walk continues up the hill ahead, Mont Sohier, and thence directly back to Deloraine Road, crossing Rue à la Dame into Les Chasses crowned with a fine row of trees until the 1987 hurricane—(Les Caches; Bel Air Lane). The strip of land on the left of Les Chasses is a fine example of an *issue*, a strip of land originally forming part of the land on the other side of the road and left isolated when the road was made. The part adjoining the Le Geyt Homes went with the land on which the Homes are built, and Miss Le Geyt bought the remainder so as to ensure that the strip should remain wooded. One hopes that the position may yet be restored and her wishes met.

Walk 22

2 miles (3.2 km)

Les Petits Vaux

Start: In Vallée-des-Vaux, just beyond La Pouquelaye steps; SO
Map ref. 651 506
There is one moderately steep hill.

Between the town of St. Helier and the north coast lie two
valley complexes. Their waters used to supply the Town Mills,
which now only exist as a place name, for they were burnt
down in 1895. The main valleys of one complex rise in the high
lands bounded by Rozel Bay on the east and Bonne Nuit on
the west; the main valley of the other rises in the parish of St
John, north of the Trinity Vingtaine des Augrès. One is a great
complex, the great valleys, Les Grands Vaux; the other is a
small one, the little valleys, Les Petits Vaux. The main valley of

this complex, Vallée-des-Vaux, is the starting place for this walk.

Enter the valley at the foot of Trinity Hill. In about a quarter of a mile the road makes an S bend, and on the right is the mill pond (now dry) which used to serve the Town Mills. On the other side of the road are wooded slopes (interrupted by a couple of houses), the gift of which led to the establishment of The National Trust for Jersey. The road verges are the property of the parish of St. Helier, the authorities of which have created pleasant, though small, public gardens on the east side of the road.

Next come La Pouquelaye steps and, beyond them, two more National Trust properties (with a private house between), on the second of which an arboretum has been established. Opposite is the gorse-covered slope of La Commune des Mélèches. This is the area in which to park your car.

Set out up the valley, along which the damage of the 1987 hurricane is slowly being repaired. You will come to another National Trust property, a long stretch of land opposite the Harvest Barn, whose buildings incorporate a former water mill, Nicolle Mill.

Continue up the valley past the Harvest Barn. Shortly, two roads lead off uphill to the left and then a road leads off uphill to the right. Do not take any of these, but go straight ahead. About a quarter of a mile further on, the road rises sharply just after it has crossed the valley brook. On the left, on the far side of the brook, is an unusual sight for Jersey, a Swiss chalet. Nearby there used to be a water mill, Augrès Mill, which was demolished over 100 years ago.

LES PETITS VAUX

The course of the brook now goes off to the north and it is no longer possible to follow it. Continue up the hill till you reach a T junction, on the right of which is a fine stone arch, of ancient material, but of fairly recent construction. The stones of the arch (the remains of a double archway) were found incorporated in the random stonework of a roadside wall. The property to which the arch gives entrance is Bras de Fer, named after Guillaume Bras de Fer who, in 1331, was Seigneur des Augrès in right of his wife (in those days, and until 25 April 1925, the enjoyment of a woman's real property passed to her husband on her marriage). This has long since ceased to be the site of Augrès Manor, which came to be established on the Fief de Diélament and now houses the Jersey Zoo.

Now turn to the right and go down the road until a lane leading off to the right is reached. Opposite the entrance to the lane, set into the foot of the bank, is a parish road boundary stone on two faces of which are inscribed the letters TN^t and on another the letters S^{t}H denoting the parishes of Trinity and St Helier.

At this point, take the lane on the right. Shortly there is an S bend and in about 100 yards, just before the lane begins to descend steeply, you will find an entrance on the left through which you pass to reach a track. Further on, the surface becomes tarmac and the lane ends at La Rue du Petit Clos.

Take the road to the right descending the hill which, after winding to the left and then to the right, borders on La Commune des Mélèches. The Common is on the left, and where the road curves to the right, there is a path leading on to it. The path immediately divides, and the left-hand branch, which at first rises steeply, crosses the entire length of the Common and will lead you towards your starting place.

Walk 23   From Grève d'Azette to Gorey
6¹/₂ miles (10.5 km)

Start: The Dicq slipway; SO Map ref. 659 477

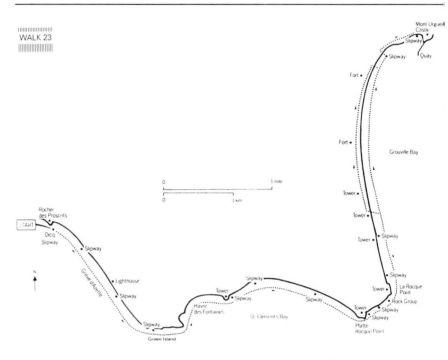

This walk takes you along beaches. Most of the beaches are covered at high tide, and to be safe, it is best to set out when the tide is receding. If the tide is rising, make sure that you have a means of escape from the beach.

Beach surfaces can quickly be changed by the tides. You may therefore find them in a somewhat different state from that described, especially between Seymour Tower and the coastal road where there have latterly been heavy deposits of sand.

The Dicq slipway is at the western end of Grève d'Azette, and to start from here, leave your car at the car park at the intersection of St Clement's Road and La Route du Fort.

The walk is described as a continuous one from Grève d'Azette to Gorey, mainly along the beach. To return, you will have either to retrace your steps or to travel by bus along the Coast Road.

You may, however, like to do part only of the route. If so, you will find car parks at La Mare Slipway, Green Island, Le Hocq, La Rocque Harbour, the eastern end of Grouville Common and Gorey Harbour.

Grève d'Azette The great rock above the Dicq is called Le Rocher des Proscrits after Victor Hugo and his fellow *proscrits*—inveterate enemies of the Emperor Napoleon III— who sought refuge in Jersey and used to foregather here, not far from Victor Hugo's home.

One is able to walk on firm sand for most of the length of Grève d'Azette, though the surface tends to be covered in parts

GREVE D'AZETTE BEACH

with a damp film. Towards the eastern end of the bay, the beach is as fine as any can be, firm and generally drying out as soon as the sea recedes.

The lighthouse on shore in the middle of the bay, Grève d'Azette Lighthouse, serves as one of the navigation marks of the sea approach to St Helier Harbour from the west.

At the far end of the bay is La Motte or Green Island, containing a stone age burial place where a complete skull of a type common to the new stone age races, and other remains, were discovered in 1911.

St Clement's Bay   From Green Island to La Rocque is not easy going. It is possible to round the point (Le Nez) beyond Green Island Slipway at low tide, but the way, when not rocky, is over very damp ridged sand. Nor is the going entirely easy when you have rounded the point, for there is a certain amount of coarse soft sand and shingle.

The true name of the bay at the Le Hocq end of St Clement's Bay is Le Havre des Fontaines, a name derived from the fact that fresh water springs are to be found there.

At the end of Le Havre des Fontaines is Le Hocq Tower, where you have the choice of taking to the land or crossing the rocks below the tower. From there the way is over firm, damp sand, much scattered with shingle, to arrive at Pontac.

At first the beach still consists of firm and fairly dry sand with a scatter of shingle and stone, but the going deteriorates leaving a choice between very rough shingle and damp ridged sand.

The bay ends at Platte Rocque where the point is rounded through a small sandy bay behind La Rocque Harbour. You are now on the scene of part of the Battle of Jersey. Cross into the

DE RULLECOURT'S LANDING, PLATTE ROCQUE

harbour bay and observe the channel between the rocks leading out to sea. (The higher the tide, the less visible is the channel.) It was up this channel that, on the night of 5-6 January 1781, the fleet of Baron de Rullecourt came, not without losses, to land at Platte Rocque and capture an unmanned battery which, later in the day, was recaptured.

Beyond the slipway at the far end of the bay, the going becomes bad—shingle, stone and rocks, and where there is sand, it is very wet and bumpy—but continue ahead if you wish to round the south east corner of the Island; you will not round any other corner of Jersey with such ease.

There are two flights of steps built into the sea wall, and when about 20 yards beyond the foot of the second flight, do not fail to notice a group of three rocks which could pass as a modern sculpture of father, mother and child.

The line of the coast curves away to La Rocque Point where a small clump of rocks below the sea wall, called Baragone, marks the southeast corner of Jersey.

CAUTION: Do not be tempted to walk out to Seymour Tower—the square tower offshore to the east of La Rocque

Point—without an experienced local guide; unusual tides make this area very dangerous.

STATE OF THE TIDE AT LA ROCQUE

Grouville Bay Just beyond La Rocque Point stands tower No. 1 of Grouville Bay, with a guard house on its landward side. This is the area of Le Boulevard de la Rocque, the La Rocque Bulwarks, where nine militiamen on guard failed to notice the landing of Baron de Rullecourt and his troops at Platte Rocque.

There are four more towers of identical pattern in Grouville Bay, the next three, Keppel, Le Hurel and Fauvic, all having been converted for use as dwellings in the early part of this century. Originally planned as summer residences, they are now occupied all year.

As far as Fauvic Tower (tower No. 4) the going is adequate, but you may then prefer to take to the promenade along the top of the sea wall. The beach gives you the choice of damp sand or shingle and the promenade gives you the opportunity of seeing tower No. 5 which differs from the other four in having a brick sided parapet.

At the end of the promenade you will come to Grouville Common which extends as far as Gorey Village. The edge of the Common provides a very pleasant walk, but you may prefer to go along the beach whose surface varies (depending on its treatment by the sea) from very good to mediocre.

There used to be a sixth tower (numbered 8 as Fort Henry and Fort William, the two forts on the Common, were the 6th and 7th fortifications in the bay) about 100 yards to the south of Gorey Village Slipway. It stood on the boundary of the parishes of Grouville and St Martin and the walls of its platform can be seen fronting the beach. A print of 1870 shows that its parapet, like that of tower No. 5, was of brick.

Return to the shore by Gorey Village Slipway, from the head of which you will find your way through public gardens to Gorey Pier, following the former terminal route of the Jersey Eastern Railway.

Start: West Park; SO Map ref. 644 489
This is a beach walk, see note at head of Walk 23

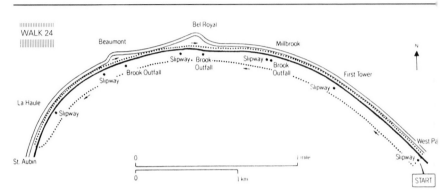

This walk is a circular one between West Park and St Aubin,
out along the beach and back by the Promenade.

There are a number of car parks at the bay and a variety of
access points to the beach. You thus have the choice of many
alternative starting places.

From West Park the sand is firm but tends to be damp until
First Tower is reached. There are odd patches of soft sand
between First Tower and Millbrook where the Mill Brook
(dividing the parishes of St Helier and St Lawrence) flows
across the beach.

Just before Bel Royal there is an unculverted outfall which is
crossable, but possible not so when the brook is in spate.
Where the granite sea wall ends at Bel Royal Slipway, you will
see a stone set into it which bears the date 1904. Here the
surface is rather damp, but afterwards the going is good over
firm sand.

About 400 yards beyond the slipway, you will come to a

brook. Called Le Douet du Canard (the Drake's Brook), it flows through Goose Green Marsh and forms the boundary between St Lawrence and St Peter.

In another 200 yards the slipway at Beaumont is reached, with tower No. 3 beyond. Then comes a culverted outfall around which the sand is very soft. The beach soon recovers its firm surface and the going continues to be good until well past La Haule Slipway.

There are two flights of steps between La Haule Slipway and St Aubin, both of which lead onto the Promenade. The first is about 200 yards beyond the slipway. Further on the beach becomes green and greasy, but by mounting the ramp below the sea wall, you should, without difficulty, reach the second flight of steps opposite the Roman Catholic Church just before the wall curves towards the harbour.

The Promenade encircling St Aubin's Bay follows the course of the railway which was closed in 1936, but although the line has gone, the station names remain attached to places round the bay where they were situated.

At the beginning of the 19th century there was neither road nor railway along the shoreline between St Aubin and La Haule, the only way to proceed dry-shod at high tide being over the hill through St Aubin High Street. The road subsequently constructed along the shore was planned for modification at the end of the 19th century as the western end of a Marine Parade which was to circle St Aubin's Bay between St Helier and St Aubin, and for which all the necessary foreshore was bought before the century was over. It was perhaps in anticipation of the completion of this project that the road came to be named Victoria Road.

On the east side of the first slipway after St Aubin, at the foot of La Haule Hill, was La Haule Station. The granite sea wall running from St Aubin continues for 200 yards or so and at its end is a very short length of German anti-tank wall. Just beyond is a line of boulders which during stormy weather were sometimes cast on to the railway line by the force of the waves, bringing the train service to a halt. The delay in the completion of the Marine Parade resulted in the lack of a sea wall between this point and Bel Royal. The Germans filled the gap, but with a wall designed to repel armed forces rather than the sea.

There used to be three towers, along the shore of St Aubin's Bay and, numbered from east to west, that at Beaumont is the third. Beaumont Station was a little further on, just beyond the slipway.

Nearing Bel Royal (where Victoria Avenue turns inland) there is a sudden broadening of the terrain, part laid out in grass and part used as a car park, for this is land which would

BETWEEN LA HAULE AND BEAUMONT

114

have been incorporated in the Marine Parade if the project for its building had been completed.

The second tower, which stood at Bel Royal, was destroyed by the Germans during the Occupation and no trace of it remains.

When you reach Millbrook, you will see the only railway building extant between St Helier and St Aubin, which is not really surprising as at all the stations, except St Helier, Millbrook, St Aubin and Corbière, the buildings were of wood.

Set into the inner side of the sea wall about 100 yards further on is a stone laid in 1901 which marks the boundary between the parishes of St Lawrence and St Helier. If you look over the sea wall, you will see the culvert of the Mill Brook which separates the two parishes.

Next comes La Ville ès Nouaux, a name now forgotten which has been superseded by 'First Tower', for here is the first tower of St Aubin's Bay. Like the other two towers of the bay, it used to stand close to the shore. It now stands inland, not because it has been moved, but because of the recovery of land from the sea for the construction of Victoria Avenue. Surplus land was ceded to the owners of the adjoining properties subject to a number of conditions, and thus one finds roadside railings of uniform design and colour, no vehicular accesses, and no buildings within 60 feet of the Avenue.

The pillar surmounted by a crown at the eastern end of the Lower Park commemorates the opening, on 22 June 1897, of the New Boulevard between Cheapside and First Tower, Victoria Avenue. (Cheapside was then what is now called Pierson Road.)

Start: L'Ouaisné; SO Map ref. 595 476
This is a beach walk, see note at head of Walk 23

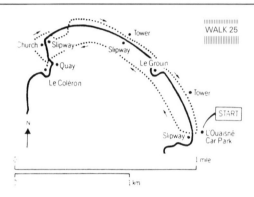

There are four flights of steps, a steep path at the western end
of the bay and a short climb over Le Grouin.

St Brelade's Bay is generally thought of as two bays—St
Brelade's Bay to the west and L'Ouaisné (normally called
Ouaisné) to the east. Actually it is a single bay with St
Brelade's Church at the western end and L'Ouaisné at the
eastern end, and in the middle a promontory called Le Grouin,
which in 12th-century French means promontory.

The walk starts from the car park at L'Ouaisné and goes
across the beach to the western end of the bay, returning
within the shoreline.

The whole of the bay is sandy, much of the sand in the
eastern half being constantly moist, but despite this and
occasional shallow pools, the surface is generally firm and the
going is good.

OUAISNÉ COMMON

Le Grouin and the western half of the slope at the rear called Le Côtil du Grouin, a heavily wooded habitat of red squirrels until the hurricane of October 1987, are public property and measure over 15 vergees (between $6^1/_2$ and $6^3/_4$ acres). The land was acquired by the States of Jersey in 1856 for use as a firing range for troops of the regular army and of the 5th or South-West Regiment of the Jersey militia. When you have passed the promontory, you will see a high winged wall in random granite. This is the only remaining evidence of the existence of the range. It seems that firing took place from the beach and that the land was bought for the purposes of safety.

When you reach the western end of the bay, go to the jetty, taking care not to trip over the mooring chains and ropes likely to be lying in your way. Pass the foot of a flight of steps on your right and continue to another flight of steps at the landward end of the jetty. These steps and the path which follows lead to the site of a former gun battery, Le Coléron, now the property of the National Trust for Jersey.

117

Return to the first flight of steps, at the top of which there is a steep path leading to the highway. At the end of the path, turn right downhill and enter St Brelade's churchyard by the west gate.

A visit to St Brelade's Church and the Fishermen's Chapel alongside is recommended. There are some items of interest in the churchyard also, such as a beautiful bronze statue of a small boy angel clasping a fish, which stands on a grave within the wall 20 yards or so to the north of the west gate. The grave of the Pipon family, at one time Seigneurs of Noirmont, stands within railings against the wall to the south of the church. It is nothing much to look at, except for its inscription which says all that needs to be said—'Pipon of Noirmont'.

Leave the churchyard by the principal entrance at the north-east corner. The parish notice box is on one side of the gateway and on the other side is the poor box bearing the inscription 'Jésus prenait garde comment le peuple mettait de l'argent au tronc' (Jesus beheld how people cast money into the treasury).

The walk continues along the promenade at the top of the sea wall, actually an anti-tank wall built by the Germans during the Occupation. Return to the beach by the slipway at the side of the churchyard gate; the second flight of steps from the slipway, about 250 yards along the beach, leads to the promenade.

Some two-thirds of the way along the promenade, you will pass tower No. 2 of St Brelade's Bay, painted black and white in chequers as a land mark.

At the end of the promenade, mount the steps to Le Côtil du Grouin, to the right of which is the random granite winged wall already mentioned.

Find your way to the top of the hill immediately ahead either by going up the steep slope in front of you or by taking the easier path to the right. From the top of the hill, follow the path which descends to the eastern half of the bay and, at its foot, passes over and at the side of a German casemate.

The tower which you see before you—tower No. 1 of St Brelade's Bay—is called La Tour du Hoinet, a name obviously linked with L'Ouaisné, but which of the two names Le Hoinet and L'Ouaisné came first is at present unknown. The tower serves as a landmark, painted as it is with red and white horizontal bands.

The path continues as a track within the sea wall (another German anti-tank wall) and from here to a point just beyond the tower it crosses private property. There is no right of way along this stretch of path, but the owners have kindly consented to its use by walkers, unless circumstances require the withdrawal of this authority. Please keep to the track and do not stray to its inland side.

6¹/₂ miles (10.5 km)

Start: La Pulente; SO Map ref. 562 489
This is a beach walk, see note at head of Walk 23

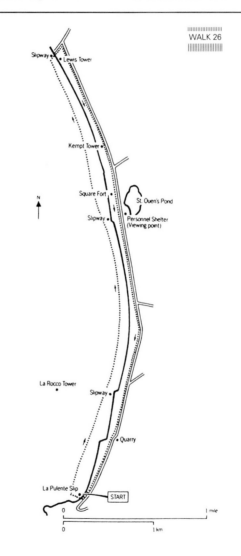

Although this article describes the walk as going along the beach from La Pulente to Les Laveurs Slipway and returning by the footpath along La Route des Mielles (the Five Mile Road), there is however the option of returning to the shore before Les Laveurs is reached or of going to a car park further up the bay and starting the walk from there.

Parking space is to be found at the head of La Pulente Slipway and also up the road on the landward side.

The going along the beach is generally good; soft sand may be encountered in places, but nothing of any consequence.

The feature of the bay is La Rocco Tower, the structure of which is so sound that although sustaining heavy damage, it withstood use as a target for gun-firing practice by the Germans during the Occupation. As the result of an appeal launched in 1969, it has been restored. La Rocco Tower, and four others of the same design, were built in St Ouen's Bay at the end of the 18th century when the ever-present danger of invasion by the French was particularly strong. All four were close to the shore; three have long since disappeared, one at least having been destroyed by the force of the sea. The fourth, at the head of L'Ouzière Slipway, was demolished by the Germans during the Occupation.

The granite sea walls are of Jersey construction; those in concrete are German anti-tank walls. Other constructions in concrete will be seen from time to time throughout this walk, giving a good idea of the extent to which Jersey was fortified by the Germans, as well as a view of a section of Hitler's Atlantic Wall.

Surf-bathing began in the early 1920s, but the sport has undergone considerable development since the War. There were no Hawaiian-type boards in the early days; body boards only were used, and if anyone thought of standing on them a successful ride was not to be expected. A result of the introduction of surfing was a rash of beach huts on the shore line. There was no building control in those days and thus nothing to stop anyone owning or able to buy or lease a plot of land from placing a hut, shack or former railway carriage on it. The Occupation brought changes; the German Army destroyed all the huts, and thanks to controls introduced in 1945, they have not been replaced.

The rocky outcrop about 750 yards beyond La Pulente Slipway is called La Carrière (The Quarry), presumably taking its name from the quarry inshore with which it is in line. The next slipway is Le Braye (*Lé Braye* is a Jersey word meaning a passage through the rocks). About a mile and a quarter further on is the slipway at L'Ouzière (at the head of which stood the tower demolished by the Germans). A walk of another mile and a quarter brings you to Les Laveurs Slipway, easily recognizable because the granite sea wall to its right is topped by a German concrete wall. At this point, return to the shore, walk up the road (La Route des Laveurs) to the place where La Route des Mielles (La Grande Route des Mielles; The Five Mile Road) takes a right-angled turn, and there go south along the footpath on the seaward side of the road.

The name La Route des Mielles dates from the time when the road was opened in 1864. The alternative name of the Five Mile Road came later, and refers to the whole length of roadway across the bay ending with La Route de l'Etacq.

The tower seen from the beach above the sea wall to the right of Les Laveurs Slipway and now to be seen to the right of the road is Lewis Tower, a martello tower of the type built also in other parts of the British Isles and in North America. The house of unusual design within a walled enclosure about 150 yards down the road was aptly named 'The Barge Aground' when built between the Wars as a summer residence.

The next in line of the early fortifications is Kempt Tower (formerly known as La Grosse Tour), after which comes the Square Fort.

On the far side of the road from the fort is Jersey's only natural fresh water of any size, St Ouen's Pond (a literal translation of the name by which it was officially known in the 17th and 18th centuries, La Mare de St Ouen). The pond belongs to the National Trust for Jersey which also owns the turf covered mound bordering the road towards the southern end of the pond. The mound was given to the Trust to serve as a viewing platform, the pond being a noted spot for wild life. It actually conceals a German-built personnel shelter where troops manning the nearby strong point could lie up when off duty. The use of banked sand sown with grass as a means of camouflage is common throughout the bay, and were it not so, it would be easier to appreciate the extent of the German fortifications.

On the seaward side of the road is the head of L'Ouzière Slipway (which is not very obvious) and further along on the same side is the National Trust for Jersey's property Le Don Hilton, a stone-roofed whitewashed building standing immediately above the sea wall. Until the 19th century, the defence of the coasts of Jersey was divided between the twelve parishes, the parishes of St Ouen and St Peter being charged with the defence of St Ouen's Bay. This was St Peter's guard house and magazine, built at the expense of the parish in 1765 in replacement of a guard house and magazine which had been blown up.

In about 700 yards, just beyond a dwelling-house on the seaward side, there is a small car park opposite a road junction. From here the western end of the runway of St Peter's Airport can be seen at the top of the hill directly to the east. Somewhat to the north is the dam of Val de la Mare Reservoir and further to the north the white tower of St Ouen's Mill appears above the top of the hill, with the steeple of St Ouen's Church to its right. Both of these were landmarks; superstitious seamen used to call the steeple Lé Mèrtcheux (possibly derived from *mèr* = a mark) because the mention of a church steeple was thought to bring ill luck.

About half a mile further along the road is the head of Le Braye Slipway and beyond it, on the landward side, a vast area of sand dunes which used to be a military exercise ground.

Walk 27
3³/₄ miles (6 km)

The Corbière Walk

Start: Old Corbière Station; SO Map ref. 556 481

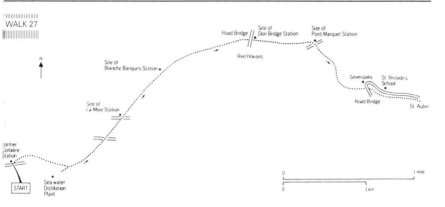

This walk is along the St Aubin to Corbière section of the railway which ran from St Helier and which closed in 1936. The description opens at Corbière and ends at St Aubin, but a number of options are open to you.

The general run is downhill to St Aubin. However, should you decide to take a walk in the opposite direction, you will find that the going is easy.

Suggested options are to walk from Corbière to St Aubin and take a bus back to Corbière; to walk from Corbière to St Aubin (or part of the way there) and back again; or to park your car at Red Houses, Pont Marquet or St Aubin and walk part of the track and back again.

Within the former railway station at Corbière is a great block of red granite called La Table des Marthes. There is no written account of the stone earlier than 1850 when excavations were briefly carried out and fragments of coarse pottery, burnt stones, cinders and broken stone axes were found. In the days

125

of the railway, it lay between the lines of the run-around loop used by the locomotive to change from one end of the train to the other.

Some way out of Corbière you will come to pillars and chains across the walk, guarding a track which crosses it Shortly afterwards, the walk curves to the left and a path comes in on the right.

RAILWAY WALK

The walk now becomes heavily lined on either side with conifers, forming a tunnel which would have been detrimental to the running of the railway. In fact, the conifers which are to be found in this area and down towards St Aubin result from tree-planting exercises carried out since the First World War, those along the walk having, of course, been planted after the closure of the railway. From here also the walk enters a belt of fertile soil between the wind-swept plateau of Corbière and the sandy waste of the aptly-named Blanches Banques.

The first highway to be crossed is that leading to Petit Port and shortly afterwards the road to La Pulente is reached. On the left, immediately after the La Pulente road crossing, stood the first station after Corbière, La Moye, where trains stopped only on request.

The deciduous trees which line the walk from the La Pulente crossing eventually come to an end and the dunes of Blanches Banques appear. The roadway leading from Route Orange to La Moye Golf Club is soon reached, but there is nothing to indicate the site of the station, Blanches Banques. This was another request stop, little used by any but golf players.

The next road crossing is at Red Houses where the walk passes under Don Bridge, a name by which the district was also known in the days of the railway. As you pass under the roadway, you will see that the original brick-vaulted bridge has been widened on the Corbière side. The station was beyond the bridge and had a passing loop. It was the only station of importance between St Aubin and Corbière, and while there were not many houses in the immediate vicinity, it served St Brelade's Bay, as well as St Peter's Barracks, now demolished, whose site is incorporated within the Airport.

The walk has now begun to descend the valley at the mouth of which lies the town of St Aubin.

A little under half a mile from Don Bridge was Pont Marquet Station, another request stop, on the left just before the road crossing. Behind the site of the station, you can see the embankment constructed by the Germans during the Occupation for their railway line connecting with branches to St Ouen's Bay and Ronez Quarries. This is a red squirrel area, as you may see from nibbled conifer cones underfoot. Their

BELOW PONT MARQUET

habitat was so depleted after October 1987 that further up the Pont Marquet Road squirrels seeking food were being run over in such numbers that the authorities built a 'squirrel bridge', linking trees on opposite sides, so that they might cross in safety.

Beyond the high bridge at Seven Oaks by which Mont les Vaux (St Aubin's Hill) is carried over the walk is a level crossing, on the left of which is a pillar showing another name for the hill—Route de St Brelade. A little way up the hill on the far side, you will see the old St Brelade's School, with doors in the centre of the bay windows, for the story goes that when the building had been erected, it was realised that no provision had been made for entrance doors and the bay windows had to be used to make good the deficiency.

Further on a path on the right leads to the railway tunnel which is now blocked, having been used by the Germans during the Occupation as an entrance to further tunnels which

BRIDGE AT SEVENOAKS

have since been put to use partly as a miniature rifle range and partly as a Telephone Department store. The path follows the original course of the railway line before the tunnel was constructed and leads down into the town of St Aubin.

Here, in the days of the railway, the train crossed in front of the Market (the open part of which has now been set out as an ornamental garden) in a tight curve, with screeching wheels and at a snail's pace, to reach the through platform on the sea side of the station buildings which incorporated the Terminus Hotel. After devastation by fire in October 1936, the train sheds, platforms and other buildings were demolished, leaving the hotel which has since been converted for use as St Brelade's Parish Hall.

Walk 28   Corbière

3 miles (4.8 km)

Start: Old Corbière Station; SO Map ref. 556 481

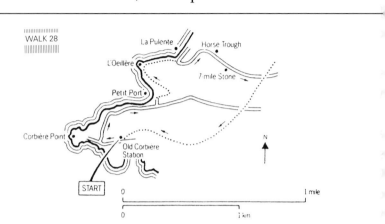

Park your car in the open space between the road and the station and proceed downhill towards Corbière lighthouse. The working of the lighthouse is now fully mechanised. No longer do lighthouse keepers in times of fog set detonators against a great iron shield and fire them at half-hour intervals, thereby providing a warning to shipping supplementary to the bell which sounded three times in quick succession at intervals of ten seconds. The fog signal (which, at the time of writing is a diaphonic blast of five seconds every minute) is supplemented by a radio beacon which also transmits wind direction, force and maximum gust experienced at the lighthouse.

The Corbière headland was heavily fortified by the Germans during the Occupation. Much of their work remains evident, and none more so than the observation tower which now serves as the Harbour Radio Station.

Some way out to sea to the north is a very noticeable double-headed rock called La Froutchie, derived from the Jersey word *fourtchi* or *froutchi* meaning forked.

You come here to a *fourtchie* in the road. The left fork leads down to the lighthouse causeway, with cottages at the landward end built to house lighthouse keepers, but, because of mechanisaton, no longer required for that purpose.

St Ouen's Bay now comes into view, and standing on the southwest corner of the Island, you can see practically the whole of the west coast.

Take the right fork which descends through a rock cutting and later passes between high rocks and by the head of a slipway. The widened road ahead is a reminder of the German Occupation. It was then the policy of the insular authorities to create work for the local labour force as an alternative to working for the Germans. Work thus created included the widening of this carriageway, and the work was carried out with such enthusiasm that the boundary stones between the properties on the landward side of the road were removed and ettisoned, an act which, in normal times, is regarded as highly unlawful.

The road descends gently to Petit Port where you turn left towards the slipway.

The walk continues along the footpath around the headland, the peak of which is called L'Oeillière (the eye-tooth). The entrance to the footpath is to be found to the right of the road to the slipway and can be recognized by the three tall concrete pillars which bar it. The path winds and follows the side of Petit Port. Corbière Lighthouse comes more and more into view, and after the path has taken a turn to the right and proceeded slightly uphill, quite extensive German fortifications are to be seen at the point of the headland. From here, Guernsey and Sark, with Herm and Jethou in between, can be seen on the horizon to the north when the air is sufficiently clear. St Ouen's Bay comes into full view, the German anti-tank wall at the head of the beach at La Pulente being particularly noticeable.

When you reach the highway, proceed uphill. About 100 yards beyond the final curve of the hill, you come to a horse trough, dated 1868, on the left of the road, one of several built in the latter half of the 19th century—grander versions of the *abreuvoirs* to be seen on other walks. About 150 yards further on, at the right of the entrance to Le Parcq de l'Oeillière on the other side of the road, is a seven-mile stone. This is the last in a series of peculiar interest as they follow a route through St Brelade's Bay and above Beau Port, that being the shortest way here before Route Orange (the road west out of Red Houses) was opened in 1822.

About 400 yards further on, the road crosses the Corbière Walk. Turn right into the walk, which is heavily lined with trees and soon crosses La Route du Petit Port. Continue along the walk which is crossed by two farm tracks and divides about 100 yards beyond the second track. The branch to the left is the route of the original railway line which led also to the quarries now housing the Waterworks Company's sea water distillation plant, whose chimney is to be seen through the trees to the left. Your course, however, is along the branch to the right where St Ouen's Bay comes increasingly into view.

At Corbière Station, note the old railway platform and the large block of red granite in the centre of the track called La Table des Marthes (see p. 125).

Walk 29   **Around Mont Ubé**

2¹/₂ **and 3 miles (4 and 4.8 km)**

Start: La Blinerie, St Clement; SO Map ref. 675 476
There is a steep hill shortly after the beginning of the walk

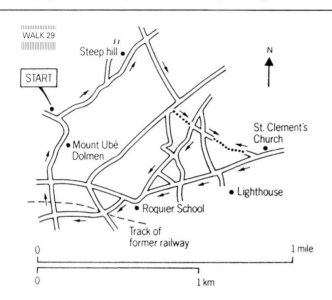

La Blinerie is the road which runs from the junction of Plat
Douet Road and Victoria Road, Georgetown, behind the Jersey
Recreation Grounds and Samarès Manor, passing the mouth of
a road (La Rue du Coin) on the left, and emerging, after a
right-angled turn, on St Clement's Inner Road at the head of
Samarès Lane.

Park your car in La Blinerie on the townward side of the
mouth of La Rue du Coin.

Set off down La Rue du Coin and in about 200 yards you
will come to a parish road boundary stone set into the top of
the bank on the right of the road. The stone is of unusual shape
for, instead of being square, it is broad and comparatively thin.

133

The incised letters StC and Gle indicate the parishes of St Clement and Grouville.

The road winds and then turns to the left, shortly after which a hill road comes in on the right of the road. Mount this hill—it is a fairly stiff climb—and take the first turning to the right into a lane which continues uphill. It eventually flattens out to arrive at a T junction where there is a fine view of St Clement's Bay with Icho Tower in the centre. The name of the rock on which the tower is built provides an example of variations in the Jersey language, for in the west of the Island 'echo' is *écho* as in French, while here the word is *icho*.

Now turn to the right and in about 100 yards you will come to a footpath and a lane, La Rue de Genestet, on the left of the road. The walk continues along the footpath which emerges on a hill road and, across it, continues as a narrow road which in turn emerges on another hill.

The narrow road continues ahead. In about 50 yards there is a view to the right of Le Mont de l'Eglise (Church Mount) and an inland lighthouse. This has a companion lighthouse on the shore at Grève d'Azette, the two lights being leading lights of the western passage to St Helier's Harbour.

Directly before you the spire of St Clement's Church shows over the hill with La Rocque Point and Grouville Bay beyond. In clear weather the French coast will be seen on the horizon.

The lanes and paths in this area used to be known as 'the dead lanes', showing that they were *chemins de corps* (*c'mins d'corps*) along which funeral processions passed on their way to St Clement's Church.

The narrow road now becomes a footpath again and after a twist descends towards the church which, when the path ends, comes into full view. A short length of narrow road will bring you to St Clement's Inner Road between the church and the

Priory Inn, a name which calls to mind the Priory of Pierreville in the parish of St Clement.

ST. CLEMENT'S CHURCHYARD GATE WITH STILE

The stone stile at the side of the churchyard gate is now purely decorative, but it served a useful purpose in the days when the Rector's sheep and cattle were put out to pasture in the churchyard.

To complete the tour, you have two choices. One is to go along the Inner Road; the other is to go back up the footpath and to join the Inner Road near Le Roquier School.

First alternative On emerging onto the Inner Road, turn right. Where some way ahead it takes a right-angled turn to the left, the second alternative route comes in on the right.

Second alternative The way back by the footpath has the merit that it spares you the traffic of the Inner Road. When you reach the top of the rise, the path runs level and then becomes a narrow road which, after a short descent, continues across a road coming downhill from the right. The narrow road continues to descend and shortly meets another hill road, where you turn left downhill.

When you reach a road, La Rue de Genestet, coming in on your right, turn into it and almost immediately turn left into La Rue du Presbytère which takes its name from St Clement's Rectory on the right of the road just before it levels out.

The routes reunited   Where La Rue du Presbytère emerges on to St Clement's Inner Road, the first alternative route comes in on the left.

Continue ahead. Shortly there is a right-angled turn to the right, and in about 100 yards a road, La Rue de la Chapelle, going off to the left. The walk continues down this road.

The road emerges to cross Pontorson Lane (La Rue de Pontliétaut) and the track of the former Jersey Eastern Railway; it continues as La Rue de la Croix. The track of the railway is easily distinguishable. On the right on the far side stands the dwelling which housed the gate-keeper of the level crossing.

On your left as you enter La Rue de la Croix is a large open garage at the side of The Hollies. Here, bordering the road, was a double arched entrance gateway which, after its demolition, was re-erected at the entrance to Mont Pellier, Trinity, in the lane which leads south from Trinity Church, across the valley from Trinity School. It is to be seen soon after the start of Walk 6.

Further on, on the same side of the road, there is a mounting block outside Ivy-Stone.

136

At the end of La Rue de la Croix, turn right into Samarès Lane and proceed up the lane, passing on the left the former Samarès station of the Jersey Eastern Railway, where the station house is still to be seen. There was real uniformity in the design of the railway buildings. Four other station houses survive—those at Le Hocq, Fauvic, Grouville and Gorey Village. Not only were the station houses of a standard pattern, but the hand of the same designer was also noticeable in most of the other railway buildings which, with few exceptions, were given a smooth cement finish.

At the top of Samarès Lane, cross St Clement's Inner Road into La Blinerie where, on the way back to your car, you will pass a wooded slope on the right belonging to the National Trust for Jersey. At the top of the slope is Mont Ubé Dolmen, the property of the Société Jersiaise, which is well worth visiting.

Start: La Rocque Harbour; SO Map ref. 706 465

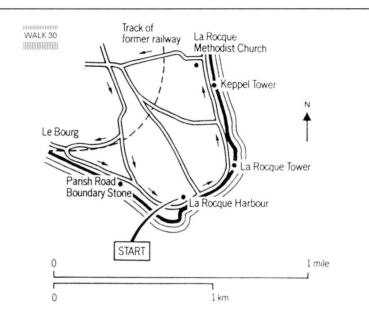

This walk begins at La Rocque Harbour where there is a car park between the slipways.

The harbour quay is built out from Platte Rocque (not to be confused with La Rocque Point to which you will be coming later in this walk). Here, at high tide, hardly a rock is to be seen. The tide recedes to uncover Le Banc de Vielet dominated by La Tour de la Grande Avarizon, commonly called Seymour Tower, about 1 ¹/₄ miles from the shore, and a great bank of rocks appears intersected by gullies, one of which leads from the open sea to Platte Rocque. It was up this gully that Baron de Rullecourt landed to invade the island on the night of the 5-

138

LA ROCQUE GUARDHOUSE AND TOWER

6 January 1781, unobserved by the guard posted at La Rocque Point (see p. 109).

Set out towards Gorey. When the roadway and the sea wall are about to part company, look ahead along the line of the sea wall and at its extreme end you will see the tip of the rock called Baragone at La Rocque Point, the south-east corner of Jersey. Continuing along the road, you will come to cottages which take their name from the rock, indicating that you are turning the corner between the south and east coasts.

You are now in the area of Le Boulevard de la Rocque. *Boulevard* means bulwark—a work of protection or defence. That at La Rocque was one of the many fortified places in Jersey which were maintained throughout the centuries in a state of repair varying according to the threat of invasion by the French. The bulwarks extended from La Rocque Point almost as far as the house called Grenville, and all that now remains are the guard house and tower where troops were posted to guard the coast.

La Rocque was an area much favoured at the turn of the century for the country residence of the St Helier business man, and some of the houses which you see here were built at that time and for that purpose. Facing the sea, they are fully exposed to the cold easterly winter winds, but they were designed as summer residences and were never intended to be lived in during the winter. Note, by contrast, how the older houses present their gables to the sea. But times have changed, and central heating and double glazing make good the lack of protection by a stout gable.

Further along the road is tower No. 2 of Grouville Bay (Keppel Tower), one of the three towers of the bay which have been adapted as a dwelling. 250 yards or so beyond, there is a mounting block on the right of the farm entrance just before La Rocque Methodist Church.

The walk continues down the lane on the left which soon takes a turn to the right and a turn to the left. A little way further on there is a single-storeyed dwelling on the left called La Sente Cottage. This originally housed the gate-keeper of the Jersey Eastern Railway level crossing located here, whose gates are still in position despite the lapse of some 50 years since the closure of the railway.

Continue ahead beyond the end of the lane and on arriving at a crossroads turn to the left into La Rue de la Lourderie. When you come to a lane on the right, La Petite Sente, look to the left and the right immediately beyond the lane and you will clearly see the track of the Jersey Eastern Railway. There was never any gate-keeper's house at this point, the crossing being closed by the lowering of bars controlled by wire from La Rocque Station. The station buildings have been demolished, but its site can easily be observed, for it is occupied by the house at the far end of the track on the left.

You now have the option of continuing ahead or of turning into the lane, La Petite Sente, on the right. The two routes rejoin on the Coast Road opposite the St. Clement – Grouville boundary stone.

La Petite Sente will bring you to the Coast Road at Le Bourg. Here turn to the left up the road towards La Rocque, noting as you proceed on your way the variety of domestic architecture, much of it pleasing, which has appeared here during the last 100 years.

In due course the Coast Road curves to the right and La Rue de la Lourderie comes in on the left. Just before the junction there is a short length of wall on the right which incorporates a parish road boundary stone.

The two routes having now rejoined, the walk continues up the road towards La Rocque Harbour.

As the walk ends, you will see Platte Rocque Tower as well as the remains of German fortifications. The tower was not there when de Rullecourt landed in 1781, and no traces remain of the battery which he then captured, its site probably being occupied by the delightful granite house which stands on Platte Rocque Pointe and whose style might well be described as Victorian Gothic-Romantic.